# Amazing Visions of the Future
## —Aspects of Human Activity—

国際社会への英語の扉
―インプットからアウトプットで学ぶ四技能―

伊與田 洋之
赤塚 麻里
土居 峻
梶浦 眞由美
Marikit G. Manalang
室 淳子

NAN'UN-DO

# Amazing Visions of the Future
## —Aspects of Human Activity—

Copyright© 2019

by
Hiroyuki Iyoda
Mari Akatsuka
Schun Doi
Mayumi Kajiura
Marikit G. Manalang
Junko Muro

All Rights Reserved
No part of this book may be reproduced in any form without written permission from the authors and Nan'un-do Co., Ltd.

このテキストの音声を無料で視聴(ストリーミング)・ダウンロードできます。自習用音声としてご活用ください。
以下のサイトにアクセスしてテキスト番号で検索してください。

**https://nanun-do.com**　　テキスト番号 [ **511990** ]

※ 無線 LAN(WiFi)に接続してのご利用を推奨いたします。

※ 音声ダウンロードは Zip ファイルでの提供になります。
　お使いの機器によっては別途ソフトウェア(アプリケーション)の導入が必要となります。

※ Amazing Visions of the Future 音声ダウンロードページは以下の QR コードからもご利用になれます。

Illustrations by Yasco Sudaka (p.36, 43, 47, 67, 70)

# は　し　が　き

　グローバル社会において，英語コミュニケーション能力は，ますます必要な時代になってきています。本書は，この時代の流れに沿って，「インプットからアウトプットへ」をコンセプトにし，執筆者が知恵を出し合い，4技能を盛り込んだ総合教材として開発しています。

　英語の学習者は，ふだんの日常会話や英語のニュースなどを聞き取ったり，映画を日本語の吹き替えなしで楽しんだり，海外旅行に役立つ英語力を身に付けたいと望んでいます。さらに一歩進んで，プレゼンテーションで自分の考えを英語で述べたり，留学してコミュケーション能力を飛躍的に伸ばしたいと考えている学習者も数多くいます。このテキストはそのような人たちのために基礎固めができるよう，初級者から中級者向けの教材として，レベルに応じた語彙や表現を使うなどの配慮をしています。

　本書の特色は，学習者の視点に立って，豊富で多彩なトピックを取り上げ，その興味・関心を引き付ける工夫をしていることです。さらには，各ユニットを構成するリスニング，リーディング，ライティング，スピーキングのセクションを有機的に関連させ，一つのトピックをインプットからアウトプットへの流れの中で学習できるようにしています。例えば，リスニングはTOEIC に準じた形式を取り入れ，Exercise 3 の Opening Conversation はプレ・リーディング・アクティビティとして，リーディングへの橋渡しをしています。さらにそこに出てくる実際の会話は，使用頻度の高い表現をスピーキングで練習できるようにしています。

　様々な視点や感覚を持つ筆者たちが，学習者に幅広い知識・知見・感性を与える機会を増やすことを同じ目標として，この一冊にその思いを詰めています。本書の英語学習を通して，教養を深めるとともに，外国人のものの考え方を理解し，自分の国の文化を発信できるようになることを願ってやみません。

　最後に，本書の刊行にあたり，南雲堂編集部の丸小雅臣氏，伊藤宏実氏には有益なご助言をいただきました。ここに深く感謝の意を表します。

2019 年 2 月
執筆者一同

# 本書の構成

## 🔊 Listening　Warming up

英語の音声の聞き取りを助けるヒントを簡潔に紹介しています。語アクセント，文アクセントなどの基本的なルールから，消こえなくなる音，弱形と強形，つながる音，英語のリズムなど，英語の音声の特徴について解説しています。学習に入る前のウォーミングアップに役立ちます。

**Exercise 1**　何についての説明かを聞き取り，それを日本語で答える問題です。一語一語にこだわるのではなく，全体として，内容を捉える練習です。

**Exercise 2**　発話とそれに対する3つの応答を聴き，発話に対する最もふさわしい応答を1つ選ぶ問題です。TOEIC® L&R Test の Part Ⅱ Question – Response に対応した問題です。

**Exercise 3**　Reading Passage のトピックに関連する Opening Conversation を聞き取り，会話の内容に関する質問に答える問題です。内容を聞き取ると同時に，Reading Passage への意識付けができます。

## 📖 Reading

各ユニットのトピックに関連した題材を取り上げた 300 語前後の英文です。色々な話題を英語で考えながら，その視野を広げられるように工夫をしています。

**Exercise 1**　多項選択式で本文の内容理解を確認する問題です。

**Exercise 2**　本文の内容について真偽を問う問題です。

**トピック・コラム**　Reading Passage で取り上げたトピックに関連して，興味を喚起させるような耳寄りな情報を日本語で説明しています。トピックについてさらに知識を広げ，考察を深めるのに役立ちます。

## ✏️ Writing

**Exercise 1**　空所補充形式で，本文中に出てくる重要語句やフレーズを確認する問題です。

**Exercise 2**　語句を並べ替えて英文を完成させる問題です。最初の設問のみ日本語訳でヒントを付けています。

## 💬 Speaking

Listening の Exercise 3　Opening Conversation で出てきた重要表現を対話形式で発話して，インプットからアウトプットできる能力を養成します。

### 付録

音声学的観点から，日本語と英語の違い，強アクセントと弱アクセント，イントネーションなどを解説しています。英語らしい発音を意識し，特に，リスニング力向上やスピーキング時などにも活用できます。

# CONTENTS

| | | |
|---|---|---|
| **Unit 1** | **Goals in College Life**<br>充実した大学生活を送るには | 7 |
| **Unit 2** | **Totoro Travels to Nepal**<br>ネパールでの国際交流の体験 | 11 |
| **Unit 3** | **Sightseeing in London**<br>国際観光都市ロンドン | 15 |
| **Unit 4** | **Sushi**<br>世界が誇る和食文化 | 19 |
| **Unit 5** | **Fashion Trends**<br>ファッションを考える | 23 |
| **Unit 6** | ***Shodo***<br>書道は昔の教養科目！！ | 27 |
| **Unit 7** | **The Mississippi River**<br>アメリカ最長の河 | 31 |
| **Unit 8** | **Ocean Blue**<br>洞窟ダイビングの人気スポット | 35 |
| **Unit 9** | **Studying Abroad**<br>留学する前に考えておくべきことは | 39 |
| **Unit 10** | **The Northern Lights**<br>カナダのオーロラ観光 | 43 |
| **Unit 11** | **The Sound of the Saxophone**<br>サキソフォンの魅力的な音色 | 47 |
| **Unit 12** | **Communication Tips**<br>良好な人間関係を築くには | 51 |
| **Unit 13** | **Seasonal Festivals (*Sekku*)**<br>9月9日は菊のお節句 | 55 |
| **Unit 14** | **Electric Cars**<br>環境にやさしい車 | 59 |
| **Unit 15** | **The Amazing Brain**<br>驚異的な脳の働き | 63 |
| | **付録** | 67 |

# Unit 1
# Goals in College Life
充実した大学生活を送るには

## 🔊 Listening  Warming up

◆ 語アクセント ◆

日本語は高低のアクセントで発音され，例えば「アメ」であれば「雨」と「飴」というように，アクセントの位置によって意味が変わります。それに対して，英語は強弱のアクセントで発音されます。強弱の付け方によって違う単語になってしまうこともあるので，注意が必要です（①〜③）。また，複合語も1つの単語として強弱のアクセントが付きます（④〜⑦）。

① desert  砂漠
② desert  見棄てる
③ dessert  デザート
④ White House  ホワイトハウス
⑤ white house  白い家
⑥ blackboard  黒板
⑦ black board  黒い板

**Exercise 1**  CDを聴いて，何のアイテムの説明か，その名前を日本語で（　）内に書き入れましょう。

A (　　　　　　　)　　B (　　　　　　　)　　C (　　　　　　　)

**Exercise 2**  CDを聴いて，最も適切な応答を一つ選びましょう。

1. (A) (B) (C)　　2. (A) (B) (C)　　3. (A) (B) (C)　　4. (A) (B) (C)

**Exercise 3**  Opening Conversationを聴いて，下の質問に日本語で答えましょう。

1. Davidはどの都市から来ましたか。

2. Sayakaは大学で何を専攻していますか。

## Reading 英文を読んで，質問に答えましょう。

People go to college or university for a variety of reasons. There might be three main ones: to increase their knowledge, to make new friends, or to prepare for their future career.

First of all, university provides students with good opportunities to increase their knowledge and skills. You have to choose your specific area of study and understand your chosen subject deeply. If you are interested in politics, you will study public administration, law, the constitution, and other related fields such as economics. In order to do this, you have to attend lectures, read a lot of books, and consult with your adviser. Sometimes you need to do surveys and submit reports. Finally, you are required to complete your final project or thesis in your own subject area.

Second, many students will meet new people from other parts of the world. Your new friends may speak different languages or have different ways of life. Their different cultural backgrounds will allow you to learn more about the world and yourself. You can exchange your views and opinions with them. They will have a great impact on you. Your new friends will learn from you as well.

The final and most important thing is to get qualifications that will provide you with a future job. If you want to be a lawyer, you must have a wide range of knowledge about law, which will enable you to advise your clients. A lawyer with professional knowledge will be helpful for people experiencing legal problems. In other words, your profession will determine the role you are expected to play in society.

(267 words)

(L. 2-3) future career 将来の職業　　(L. 6) politics 政治学　　(L. 6-7) public administration 行政
(L. 7) constitution 憲法　　(L. 7) economics 経済学　　(L. 8) consult 相談する　　(L. 9) submit 提出する
(L. 10) thesis 論文　　(L. 10) subject area 専門分野　　(L. 14) view 考え　　(L. 16) qualification 資格
(L. 18) client 依頼人　　(L. 20) profession 職業

**Exercise 1**  本文を読んで，下の質問に答えましょう。

1. What do students decide when they enter university?
   - (A) Their specific study area
   - (B) Their new friends
   - (C) Their adviser
   - (D) Their professional knowledge

2. How will your new friends influence you?
   - (A) They will tell you how to achieve your goals.
   - (B) They will show you how to write an academic paper.
   - (C) They will talk about their cultural backgrounds.
   - (D) They will show you different ideas and opinions.

3. What are university graduates expected to do in society?
   - (A) To show a wider range of knowledge about society
   - (B) To have information about the law
   - (C) To help people in society
   - (D) To consult their clients' requests

**Exercise 2**  次の各文が本文の内容に合っていれば T を，合っていなければ F を選びましょう。

1. 【T / F】 If you do a lot of reading in the library, you don't have to attend lectures.

2. 【T / F】 You must do a wide variety of things in order to understand your subject area better.

3. 【T / F】 Many people go to college or university only to get a good job.

---

### ◎ ギャップ・イヤー ◎

日本では高校を卒業して，すぐ大学に進学するか，あるいは就職するかを選択することが一般的です。しかし，欧米などでは進学も就職もしないで，ギャップ・イヤーを活用する若者が数多くいます。例えば，ヨーロッパの街角でバックパックを背負って，安いホテルなどに泊まりながら，各地を見聞して回る若者を見かけることは珍しいことではありません。

# Writing

**Exercise 1** 日本語に合うように，（　）内に適切な語を書き入れましょう。

1. Universities provide students (　　　　　) opportunities for career advancement.
   （大学は学生にキャリア・アップをするための機会を与えてくれます。）

2. New students are (　　　　　) to join the orientation program next week.
   （新入生は来週のオリエンテーションへの参加を求められています。）

3. Students must have a wide (　　　　　) of knowledge in their subject area.
   （学生は自分の専門分野で広い知識を持たなければなりません。）

**Exercise 2** （　）内の語を並べ替えて，英文を完成させましょう。

1. It is important ( skills / students / good / to / note-taking / for / develop ).
   （学生が良いノートの取り方を習得することは重要です。）

   ..................................................................................................................................

2. You must try ( your / all / attend / classes / to ).

   ..................................................................................................................................

3. A college student is ( society / play / in / role / an / expected / important / to ) in his or her future.

   ..................................................................................................................................

# Speaking 次の表現を使って，パートナーと話す練習をしましょう。

| A: Where are you from? | A: What is your major? |
| B: I'm from Fukuoka. | B: My major is European Culture. |

**Exercise** 日本語に合うように，英語で表現しましょう。

1. A: Where are you from?
   B: I'm from _____.　（日本，東京，広島，自分の出身地）

2. A: What is your major?
   B: My major is _____.　（アメリカ文学，近代経済学，環境科学，自分の専攻）

# Unit 2
# Totoro Travels to Nepal
ネパールでの国際交流の体験

## 🎧 Listening  Warming up  7

◆ 文アクセント ◆
語だけではなく，文の中でも強弱があります。内容語（動詞，名詞，疑問詞など）は強く発音され，機能語（代名詞，助動詞，前置詞，冠詞，接続詞など）は弱く発音されます（付録 ② p.68 参照）。特に，話者が文中で一番伝えたい情報は最も強く発音します。

① Here comes a major earthquake.

② He's working for a trading company.

③ A dog with a hat is on the desk.

★ 最も強い部分
● 強い部分
• 弱い部分

**Exercise 1**　CD を聴いて，どの宗教の説明か，その名前を日本語で（　）内に書き入れましょう。  8

A (　　　　　)　　B (　　　　　)　　C (　　　　　)

**Exercise 2**　CD を聴いて，最も適切な応答を一つ選びましょう。  9

1. (A)　(B)　(C)　　2. (A)　(B)　(C)　　3. (A)　(B)　(C)　　4. (A)　(B)　(C)

**Exercise 3**　Opening Conversation を聴いて，下の質問に日本語で答えましょう。  10

1. Sayaka はどこに行きましたか。

2. Sayaka は何の活動をしましたか。

**Reading** 英文を読んで，質問に答えましょう。

　Last winter, Sayaka and Mary participated in an international cultural exchange program to Nepal. On February 10, many people gathered for the birthday festival of Shiba, a Hindu god. The two were very excited and could feel the atmosphere of the city through seeing the colorful costumes and the rising dust in the air.

　They visited the Bhanubhakta Memorial School. There, they showed the movie *My Neighbor Totoro* to the pupils. *My Neighbor Totoro*, a famous Studio Ghibli animation, is a classic movie suitable for all generations. It features mysterious beings called "Totoro" and shows the nonverbal communication that occurs between them and children. Hayao Miyazaki's animated films show Japanese culture through the existence of mysterious and magical creatures like "Totoro," which may be partly based on unconscious shintoistic modes of thinking. After that, the children sang "Sampo" while doing the choreography and singing the Japanese lyrics together. They had told the children about *Totoro* before coming, so the students were able to participate actively.

　Nepal is mainly Hindu and has various ethnic groups. People in Nepal are religious and have many gods. Sayaka and Mary could see how much the students naturally appreciated "Totoro" and how easy it was for the children to connect with the idea of "Totoro." Singing the song and acting out the meaning of the lyrics may also have led to a better understanding of Japanese culture.

　Although "Totoro" are far from divine, it was easy for the Nepalese children to understand the movie and the story because they are very open-minded. Sayaka and Mary were happy to share Japanese culture with the Nepalese children and they learned a lot from their cross-cultural exchange experience.

(282 words)

(L. 4) costume 衣装　　(L. 5) Bhanubhakta Memorial School バーヌバクタは，詩人の名前に由来した学校名
(L. 7) feature 特徴づける　　(L. 8) nonverbal 言葉によらない　　(L. 11) unconscious 無意識の
(L. 11) shintoistic 神道的な　　(L. 12) choreography 振付（ここでは歌詞の振付）　　(L. 12) lyrics 歌詞
(L. 16) appreciate〈人・ものの〉よさがわかる　　(L. 19) divine 神の

**Exercise 1** 本文を読んで，下の質問に答えましょう。

1. What did Sayaka and Mary do when they were in Nepal?
   - (A) They ate Nepalese cuisine. （cuisine: 料理）
   - (B) They experienced the local atmosphere.
   - (C) They climbed Mt. Everest.
   - (D) They spoke Nepali.

2. Where did they go?
   - (A) To the Shiba festival
   - (B) To the Bhanubhakta Memorial School
   - (C) To Studio Ghibli
   - (D) To the Japanese Culture Center

3. Why could the children connect with the idea of "Totoro"?
   - (A) They sang the song "Sampo."
   - (B) They watched *My Neighbor Totoro*.
   - (C) They believe in Hindu gods.
   - (D) They were very open-minded.

**Exercise 2** 次の各文が本文の内容に合っていればTを，合っていなければFを選びましょう。

1. 【T / F】 Sayaka and Mary participated in an international conference.

2. 【T / F】 They did the choreography and sang the Nepali lyrics together.

3. 【T / F】 Nepal is a Hindu country and has many ethnic groups.

---

### 🔵 日本語学校 🔵

公教育ではなく，実学的に日本語を教えています。将来，日本でビジネス，留学するために日本語を教えている学校です。ネパールには，Nepal Japan Sewa Centerがあり，主に10代から30代の人が通っています。教育プランとして，日本語の授業の他に日本文化や宗教などを学び，日本への研修活動も積極的に行なっています。

# Writing

**Exercise 1** 日本語に合うように，（ ）内に適切な語を書き入れましょう。

1. They (          ) (            ) the welcoming party for Nepalese children.
   （彼らはネパール人の子どものための歓迎会に参加しました。）

2. This story is (          ) (            ) the Japanese folk story about Princess Kaguya.
   （この物語は日本の民話"かぐや姫"に基づいています。）

3. Sayaka was (          ) (            ) happy when she met her ex-boyfriend by chance.
   （Sayaka は元彼と偶然出会った時ちっとも嬉しくありませんでした。）

**Exercise 2** （ ）内の語を並べ替えて，英文を完成させましょう。

1. She is ( and / religion / course / a / taking / philosophy / on ).
   （彼女は哲学と宗教の講義を受けています。）

   ......................................................................................................................

2. What ( population / of / the / Nepal / current / is )?

   ......................................................................................................................

3. Some ( old / features / this / of / are / town / many / its ) temples and shrines.

   ......................................................................................................................

# Speaking 次の表現を使って，パートナーと話す練習をしましょう。

> A: How was life in Nepal?
> B: It was great!
> A: Did you have a hard time introducing Japanese culture?
> B: Not really.

**Exercise** 日本語に合うように，英語で表現しましょう。

1. A: How was _____?　（昨日の天気，イチゴのアイス，春休み）
   B: It was great!

2. A: Did you have a hard time _____?
   　（外国語を勉強すること，電車で通学すること，自炊すること）
   B: Not really.

# Unit 3
# Sightseeing in London
国際観光都市ロンドン

## Listening  Warming up

◆ 聞こえなくなる音 (1) ◆

自然なスピードで話されるときは，弱くなったり，聞こえなくなったりする音があります。特定の子音が連続すると，前の単語の最後の子音が聞こえなくなることがあります。例えば，次のような例があります。

① [t] + [t]　　I've got to see it.

② [d] + [t]　　Have a good time at the party.

③ [k] + [k]　　Please give me a book case.

④ [d] + [m]　　Could you send me a letter?

**Exercise 1**　CD を聴いて，何のアイテムの説明か，その名前を日本語で（　）内に書き入れましょう。

A (　　　　　　　)　　B (　　　　　　　)　　C (　　　　　　　)

**Exercise 2**　CD を聴いて，最も適切な応答を一つ選びましょう。

1. (A)  (B)  (C)　　2. (A)  (B)  (C)　　3. (A)  (B)  (C)　　4. (A)  (B)  (C)

**Exercise 3**　Opening Conversation を聴いて，下の質問に日本語で答えましょう。

1. Sayaka はどの都市を訪ねる予定ですか。

2. David は Sayaka にどの名所を薦めましたか。

**Reading** 英文を読んで，質問に答えましょう。

　Traveling abroad can be a real adventure. Not only is it a chance to explore an unfamiliar part of the world but you get to learn and experience new things! I was able to visit the great city of London last summer. It is a truly exciting and remarkable place.

　The first site I went to was the Tower of London. Everything is wonderfully preserved and the stories behind this fortress/former prison are told with color and emotion by the Beefeaters. Beefeaters are a select group of people who serve as the tower's guardians and tour guides.

　Another beautiful and historically significant tourist attraction to visit is Buckingham Palace. The state rooms, where the Queen entertains foreign guests, are open to the public over the summer and going through these rooms is like stepping into a very large jewelry box.

　If you have read any of the Harry Potter books written by J. K. Rowling, you really should take the time to see the "The Making of Harry Potter" (Warner Bros. Studio Tour). You have to venture a little outside of London for this, but the amazing exhibits, sets, and props dedicated to the fantastic world of Harry Potter make it well worth the effort.

　There are just so many things to do in London! Aside from its rich history, it also offers a variety of opportunities to engage with its culture. Whether it's watching a play in the West End or shopping on streets lined with glittering shops, you will definitely feel London's cosmopolitan energy. And this will hopefully, in turn, fuel your motivation and curiosity for life.

(269 words)

(L. 5) fortress 要塞　(L. 8) tourist attraction 観光名所　(L. 11) jewelry box 宝石箱　(L. 14) amazing みごとな
(L. 14) exhibit 展示物　(L. 15) prop 小道具　(L. 15) dedicate 供する　(L. 15) fantastic 空想的な
(L. 17) aside from 別にして　(L. 18) engage 引き入れる　(L. 19) lined 並んだ　(L. 19) glittering きらびやかな
(L. 20) definitely 間違いなく　(L. 20) cosmopolitan 国際色のある　(L. 20) fuel かきたてる　(L. 21) curiosity 好奇心

**Exercise 1**　本文を読んで，下の質問に答えましょう。

1. Why is traveling abroad such a great opportunity?
   (A) It is a chance to see new places.
   (B) You can experience cultures that are completely different from your own.
   (C) There are so many exciting things to do and learn when you travel.
   (D) All of the above

2. Which of the following famous places was NOT included in the passage?
   (A) Buckingham Palace
   (B) The Tower of London
   (C) Tower Bridge
   (D) Warner Bros. Studios

3. Which of the following statements best describes how the author feels about London?
   (A) London is a safe but expensive city.
   (B) London is an exciting city that offers many cultural opportunities.
   (C) London is where the Queen of England lives.
   (D) London is worth visiting because it is famous.

**Exercise 2**　次の各文が本文の内容に合っていればTを，合っていなければFを選びましょう。

1. 【T / F】 The Tower of London is a former prison that has now been turned into a shopping mall.

2. 【T / F】 Buckingham Palace is a popular tourist attraction but it is only open to tourists during the summer months.

3. 【T / F】 "The Making of Harry Potter" (Warner Bros. Studio Tour) is located within the city of London.

---

### 🔵 ロンドン 🔵

ロンドンは約2,000年前，ローマ人が建設した街です。当時はロンディニウムと呼ばれていました。黒死病（ペスト）やロンドン大火など苦難な時代を経て，多様性に富む文化を積み重ねながら現在の大都市へと発展しました。ロンドン塔，ウェストミスター寺院，バッキンガム宮殿，大英博物館などが観光名所ですが，最近ではロンドン市街が一望できるロンドン・アイが人気スポットになっています。

# Writing

**Exercise 1** 日本語に合うように，( ) 内に適切な語を書き入れましょう。

1. I plan to take a trip to London next (　　　　　).
   （私は来年の夏，ロンドンに旅行することを計画しています。）

2. Many tourists (　　　　　) London every year.
   （たくさんの旅行者が毎年ロンドンを訪れています。）

3. When in London, you can take the time to (　　　　　) a play in the West End.
   （ロンドン滞在中，ウエスト・エンドで演劇を観てすごすことができます。）

**Exercise 2** ( ) 内の語を並べ替えて，英文を完成させましょう。

1. Traveling can be a chance ( a / of / world / explore / to / new / the / part ).
   （旅行は世界の新しい部分を探求する機会になるでしょう。）

   ................................................................................................................

2. Buckingham Palace is where the Queen ( official / guests / welcomes / events / and / holds ).

   ................................................................................................................

3. London is an exciting city ( because / rich / its / atmosphere / global / of / and / history ).

   ................................................................................................................

## Speaking 次の表現を使って，パートナーと話す練習をしましょう。

> A: Which places should I see in London?
> B: You should visit Big Ben, the famous clock tower.
> A: What is the best way to look for the latest travel information?
> B: You should try and check official websites on the Internet.

**Exercise** 日本語に合うように，英語で表現しましょう。

1. A: Which places should I visit in your city?
   B: You should visit _____.　（東京タワー，名古屋城，ユニバーサル・スタジオ・ジャパン）

2. A: What is the best way to travel around your city?
   B: You should try traveling by _____.　（自転車，地下鉄，市バス）

18

# Unit 4
# Sushi
世界が誇る和食文化

## 🎧 Listening  Warming up   17

◆ 聞こえなくなる音 (2) ◆

似た子音の組み合わせで，別々の単語が一つの単語のように聞こえることがあります。音がつながるとき，前の単語の子音が聞こえなくなることがあります。

① [θ] + [ð]　　Be careful wi<u>th th</u>at hot frying pan.

② [s] + [ʃ]　　My tenni<u>s sh</u>oes are outside.

③ [t] + [ð]　　I bough<u>t th</u>is yellow hat.

**Exercise 1**　CD を聴いて，何の食べ物の説明か，その名前を日本語で（　）内に書き入れましょう。  18

A (　　　　　　　)　　B (　　　　　　　)　　C (　　　　　　　)

**Exercise 2**　CD を聴いて，最も適切な応答を一つ選びましょう。  19

1. (A) (B) (C)　　2. (A) (B) (C)　　3. (A) (B) (C)　　4. (A) (B) (C)

**Exercise 3**　Opening Conversation を聴いて，下の質問に日本語で答えましょう。  20

1. Sayaka と David は，今晩何をする予定ですか。

2. アメリカで寿司が受け入れられるようになったきっかけは何ですか。

## Reading 英文を読んで，質問に答えましょう。

California rolls played an important part in making sushi popular in America. The first California rolls in the early 1970s were made with crab meat and avocado. Cucumber, mayonnaise, sesame seeds, and fish roe were added later. Interestingly, many Americans did not know they were supposed to eat the dark *nori* seaweed wrapped around rolled sushi and tried to peel it off! That is why California rolls are often prepared inside-out.

You may wonder if there is anything similar to California rolls in Japan. They were actually reimported from America and a variety of rolled sushi called *sarada-maki* has become popular in Japan.

Nowadays, there are sushi restaurants everywhere in the world. Refrigeration technology has made it easier to transport fresh seafood. People have started to enjoy food from different countries and have become more health conscious. Because of this, Japanese food has become quite popular because it is simple, healthy, and beautiful to look at.

*Washoku* was added to UNESCO's Intangible Cultural Heritage list in 2013. Traditional Japanese dishes have four attractive aspects. First, Japanese dishes use various fresh foods harvested in all four seasons. *Washoku* respects the natural taste of each ingredient and does not depend on spices and sauces. Second, *washoku* is based on a well-balanced, healthy diet. Japan has both one of the highest life-expectancy rates and one of the lowest obesity rates in the world. Third, *washoku* emphasizes how a dish is presented. *Washoku* is sometimes served with seasonal leaves or flowers and beautifully arranged in bowls and on plates. Finally, *washoku* exhibits a close connection between food and seasonal events. For example, the Japanese eat special sushi rolls called *eho-maki* on February 3 and a type of mixed rice called *chirashi-zushi* on March 3.

(290 words)

(L. 2) crab meat カニの身　(L. 3) cucumber きゅうり　(L. 3) sesame seed ゴマ　(L. 3) fish roe 魚卵
(L. 5) peel off はがす　(L. 6) inside-out 裏返しに　(L. 8) reimport 逆輸入する
(L. 10-11) refrigeration technology 冷凍技術　(L. 15) Intangible Cultural Heritage 無形文化遺産
(L. 18) ingredient 食材　(L. 19) life expectancy 寿命　(L. 20) obesity 肥満

**Exercise 1**　本文を読んで，下の質問に答えましょう。

1. What are California rolls?
   (A) Salad wraps with avocado and Californian beef
   (B) A new style of sushi without the dark *nori* seaweed
   (C) California-made sweets brought back to Japan
   (D) Arranged sushi produced in the United States

2. Why have sushi restaurants become increasingly popular worldwide?
   (A) Fresh seafood has become more available.
   (B) Students now prefer to eat out at cheaper places.
   (C) The number of Japanese tourists has increased.
   (D) Sushi restaurants have started to serve other dishes.

3. Why was *washoku* added to UNESCO's Intangible Cultural Heritage list?
   (A) *Washoku* is one of the most popular cuisines in the world.
   (B) *Washoku* does not use any spices or sauces at all.
   (C) *Washoku* is based on Japanese culture and a respect for nature.
   (D) *Washoku* includes uniquely-arranged dishes from other cultures.

**Exercise 2**　次の各文が本文の内容に合っていればTを，合っていなければFを選びましょう。

1. 【T / F】 California rolls were originally introduced into the United States by Japan.

2. 【T / F】 Japanese people generally live longer and are less obese than people in most other countries.

3. 【T / F】 Special dishes are served to celebrate seasonal events in Japan.

### ● ニューヨークでお弁当？ ●

寿司の他にも，てんぷら，すきやき，てりやきなどは海外でよく知られ，英語表現の中にも取り入れられています。今，ニューヨークではやっているのは，日本のお弁当です。お弁当カフェには，のり弁をはじめ，様々な種類のお弁当が並びます。人気の理由はやはり様々な食材がバランスよく用いられていて，ヘルシーだからです。テイクアウトが可能で手軽に利用できることも，忙しいビジネスマンたちには魅力的なようです。

# Writing

**Exercise 1** 日本語に合うように，（ ）内に適切な語を書き入れましょう。

1. She played a central (　　　　) in devising the new recipe.
   （彼女は新しいレシピの考案に中心的な役割を果たしました。）

2. (　　　　), green tea in plastic bottles is sweetened in some countries.
   （面白いことに，ペットボトルの緑茶が甘くなっている国もあります。）

3. Recently, my kids have become very (　　　　) of what they eat.
   （最近，子どもたちは食べるものを大変気にしています。）

**Exercise 2** （ ）内の語を並べ替えて，英文を完成させましょう。

1. That ( why / like / to / food / David / is / Japanese / came ).
   （そのようにして，David は和食が好きになりました。）

   ..................................................................................................................

2. I ( if / boy / ate / wonder / the ) the dishes all by himself.

   ..................................................................................................................

3. Chop up ( it / leaves / your / to / easier / lettuce / make ) to eat them.

   ..................................................................................................................

# Speaking 次の表現を使って，パートナーと話す練習をしましょう。

> A: Are you new here?
> B: Yes. I used to live in Okayama with my parents.
> A: You're always together! Have you been friends for a long time?
> B: Well, we didn't use to hang out so often.
> 　　　　　　　　　　　　　　　　　　　（hang out: 連れ立って時間を過ごす）

**Exercise** 日本語に合うように，英語で表現しましょう。

1. A: What did you like to do in your childhood days?
   B: I used to _____. （友達とサッカーをする，かくれんぼをする，人形で遊ぶ）

2. A: Is this your first time in the States?
   B: Yes. I (we) didn't use to _____.
   （たくさん旅行する，アメリカ人の友達を持つ，海外で製品を売る）

# Unit 5
# Fashion Trends
ファッションを考える

## 🎧 Listening  Warming up

◆ 弱形と強形 ◆

同じ一つの単語でも，強く発音される場合（強形）と弱く発音される場合（弱形）があります（付録③ p.69 参照）。機能語は ① 強調した時 ② 文末にくる時以外はアクセントを持たず，内容から推測しやすい場合，通常，**弱く・短く**発音されます。逆に，意味的に強調される場合には，機能語でも強形が使われます。助動詞 can, 強形の the の例を見てみましょう。

① Who <u>can</u> speak better English?　　（弱形）

　　David <u>**can**</u>.　　　　　　　　　（強形）

② This is <u>**the**</u> book I was talking about.

**Exercise 1**　CD を聴いて，何の説明か，その名前を日本語で（　）内に書き入れましょう。　　23

A (　　　　　　)　　B (　　　　　　　)　　C (　　　　　　　)

**Exercise 2**　CD を聴いて，最も適切な応答を一つ選びましょう。　　24

1. (A) (B) (C)　　2. (A) (B) (C)　　3. (A) (B) (C)　　4. (A) (B) (C)

**Exercise 3**　Opening Conversation を聴いて，下の質問に日本語で答えましょう。　　25

1. Sayaka が買い物したいものは何ですか。

2. David は何を買うかもしれないと言っていますか。

# Reading 英文を読んで、質問に答えましょう。

　Chanel, Louis Vuitton, Cristian Dior, Prada, Zara, H&M, Forever 21 and GU—how many brands do you know? What about fashion magazines such as *VIVI*, *CanCam*, and *Nylon*? If you recognize all of these names, you might be a fashionista. Your fashion possibly reflects your own unique style: street, posh, sporty, casual, or some other look.

　Students think about fashion differently, depending on the type of university they attend or the academic department they belong to. Some students are extremely conscious about fashion and will spend most of their money on fashion-related goods, including clothes, bags, shoes, hats, accessories, and cosmetics. They will often change their hairstyles depending on what look is "in" that season. Some students, however, dress more practically. For example, those who belong to university sports clubs will often wear sweatshirts and sweatpants to school.

　Fashion attitudes among students also vary across cultures. For instance, Japanese students usually dress more formally than students who attend Western universities. Most non-Japanese students tend to distinguish between daily wear and formal wear and have no problem going to school in a T-shirt and shorts, completing their look with a pair of beach sandals.

　Time, place, and occasion are also important points to consider when it comes to fashion. Another issue is whether you dress for yourself or for somebody else. What would you do if your boyfriend or girlfriend wanted you to change your style? Would you listen to them or ignore their preference? Conformity might be a priority for some, especially for younger students, but fashion is often a way for people to express themselves. So it is important to respect other people's sense of style.

(277 words)

(L. 3) fashionista ファッショニスタ（最新ファッションに敏感な人たち）　(L. 6) extremely 極端に
(L. 7) conscious 意識している　(L. 7) related 関連した　(L. 14) distinguish 区別する　(L. 20) ignore 無視する
(L. 20) preference 好み　(L. 20) conformity 調和、従順　(L. 20) priority 優先事項

**Exercise 1** 本文を読んで，下の質問に答えましょう。

1. What is a "fashionista," as described in this passage?
   (A) A person who likes cute magazines
   (B) A person who likes Chanel
   (C) A person who knows the names of brands and fashion magazines
   (D) A person who reads a lot of magazines

2. What do students who are conscious about fashion do?
   (A) They join sports clubs.
   (B) They wear sweatshirts and sweatpants to school.
   (C) They often change their hairstyles.
   (D) They always wear beach sandals.

3. Based on the passage, students' attitudes towards fashion can be based on their …
   (A) culture.
   (B) the type of university they attend.
   (C) department within their university.
   (D) all of the above

**Exercise 2** 次の各文が本文の内容に合っていれば T を，合っていなければ F を選びましょう。

1. 【T / F】 Some students who are not interested in fashion spend most of their money on fashion-related items.
2. 【T / F】 Japanese students tend to distinguish between daily wear and formal wear more than non-Japanese students.
3. 【T / F】 Time, place, and occasion are important when it comes to fashion.

---

### ○ 流行とは？ ○

流行は，購買意欲をかきたてるために押し出し式に，以前のトレンドを流行遅れにして，人為的に作られる側面もあります。例えば，流行色。"Intercolor" という国際流行色委員会では，約 2 年をかけて各国の代表が時代の流れや人々の気分にあった色の提案を行い，その中から流行色を決めています。また，パリコレなど 4 大コレクションと呼ばれるファッションショーもとても影響力があります。流行は 20 年の周期があると言われています。来年は何がはやるのでしょうか？ 20 年前の流行をヒントに観察するのも楽しいですね。

# ✏️ Writing

**Exercise 1** 日本語に合うように，（　）内に適切な語を書き入れましょう。

1. A fashionista is extremely (　　　　) (　　　　) fashion trends.
   （ファッショニスタはファッションにとても関心があります。）

2. Those who (　　　　) (　　　　) university American football clubs often wear sweatshirts and sweatpants for weight training.
   （大学のアメリカンフットボールクラブに所属している人々は，スウェットスーツを身につけて，ウエイトトレーニングをします。）

3. Non-Japanese students (　　　　) (　　　　) wear casual clothes to go to school.
   （日本人以外の学生は，学校に行くのにカジュアルな服装をする傾向にあります。）

**Exercise 2** （　）内の語を並べ替えて，英文を完成させましょう。

1. It ( important / people's / respect / sense / is / other / to ) of style.
   （他人のファッションセンスを尊重することは重要です。）

   ...................................................................................................................

2. Considering the time, place, and occasion is important when it ( to / choosing / wear / comes / what / to ).

   ...................................................................................................................

3. What would you do ( change / if / you / boyfriend / wanted / to / your ) your hair style?

   ...................................................................................................................

## 💬 Speaking　次の表現を使って，パートナーと話す練習をしましょう。

> A: Let's go shopping.　　　A: What are you going to do this weekend?
> B: Sounds good!　　　　　B: I might play tennis.

**Exercise** 日本語に合うように，英語で表現しましょう。

1. A: Let's _____!　（買い物，ランチ，テニス）
   B: Sounds good!

2. A: What are you going to do this weekend?
   B: I might _____.　（スノーボード，クラブの活動，図書館に行く）

# Unit 6
# *Shodo*
書道は昔の教養科目！！

## 🎧 Listening  Warming up

◆ 音の同化 ◆

前の音と馴染んで，音の変化が起こることがあります。音が互いに影響しあって，語尾や語頭の音が変化します。あなたは複数形の -s を発音する時に，どのように発音していますか？語尾の音が無声音（声帯が震えない音）の場合は [s]，有声音（声帯が震える音）の場合は [z] と，発音が変わります。

例：無声音の場合　① Giants　② Hawks　③ Athletics
　　有声音の場合　④ Tigers　⑤ Swallows　⑥ Dragons

**Exercise 1**　CD を聴いて，どの書道道具の説明か，その名前を日本語で（　）内に書き入れましょう。

A (　　　　　　　)　　B (　　　　　　　)　　C (　　　　　　　)

**Exercise 2**　CD を聴いて，最も適切な応答を一つ選びましょう。

1. (A) (B) (C)　　2. (A) (B) (C)　　3. (A) (B) (C)　　4. (A) (B) (C)

**Exercise 3**　Opening Conversation を聴いて，下の質問に日本語で答えましょう。

1. Mary には Kenji の作品がどのように見えましたか。

．．．．．．．．．．．．．．．．．．．．．．．．．．．．．．．．．．．．．．．．．．．．．．．．．．．．．．．．．．．．．．．．．．．．．．．．．．．．．．．．．．．

2. 今度の土曜日には Mary は何をしますか。

．．．．．．．．．．．．．．．．．．．．．．．．．．．．．．．．．．．．．．．．．．．．．．．．．．．．．．．．．．．．．．．．．．．．．．．．．．．．．．．．．．．

## Reading 英文を読んで，質問に答えましょう。

In Japan, the tradition of black and white has been passed down from old times. This contrast is said to represent all elements of the universe within a limited framework. Traditional monochrome landscape painting and the game of *go* are examples of this black-and-white cultural characteristic. The same feature can be seen in calligraphy, where what is written in black seems to show the endless universe upon white paper. You may give your feelings fresh life by expressing them in black and white.

Traditionally, calligraphy was popular among court nobles and government officials as part of their class culture and education. Being able to write in neat, well-formed handwriting was an essential requirement for promotion. Many talented officials left documents relating to their careers, which, in time, have come to be recognized as artwork. This led to calligraphy being recognized as an art form. Wang Xizhi and Chu Suiliang are among such Chinese calligraphers, and similarly respected Japanese calligraphers include Kukai and Ono no Michikaze.

Writing neatly in easy-to-read handwriting is still considered an advantage in Japanese society. This is one of the reasons why students in elementary schools have at least one calligraphy lesson every two weeks. It is also a traditional way of teaching them the structures of *kanji* and *kana*.

As a form of art, many exhibitions are held across the country, giving all calligraphers the chance to show their works. Calligraphers express their inner selves through black ink on white paper. Furthermore, preparing the ink can be a reflective and comforting experience. By changing the amount of water, you can have various shades of black, and this enables you to express different emotions. *Sho* remains a pure and mature creation of brush and ink, and is perhaps a perfect expression of Japanese sensibilities.

(297 words)

(L. 1) pass down 受け継ぐ　(L. 2) framework 枠組み　(L. 3) monochrome landscape painting 山水画
(L. 4) calligraphy 書道　(L. 7) noble 高貴な人，貴族　(L. 9) talented 才能のある　(L. 10) career 職務
(L. 11) artwork 芸術作品　(L. 11) Wang Xizhi 王羲之　(L. 12) Chu Suiliang 褚遂良　(L. 13) Kukai 空海
(L. 13) Ono no Michikaze 小野道風　(L. 14) neatly 丁寧に　(L. 20) reflective 内省的な　(L. 22) shade 影，色味
(L. 24) sensibility 感受性

**Exercise 1** 本文を読んで，下の質問に答えましょう。

1. What was traditionally essential for being promoted in ancient times?
   (A) The ability to produce artwork
   (B) The ability to prepare for exams at schools run by calligraphers
   (C) The ability to write neatly in well-formed handwriting
   (D) Being popular among court nobles and government officials

2. Why do Japanese schoolchildren practice calligraphy?
   (A) Being able to write neatly is a benefit in Japanese society.
   (B) The ability to write neatly is essential in order to get promotion.
   (C) They can learn the traditional way of teaching.
   (D) They need to present their works at exhibitions.

3. What are you able to do when you change the amount of water mixed in with the ink?
   (A) Get a thoughtful and calming experience
   (B) Express Japanese values perfectly
   (C) Present your work at exhibitions held all over Japan
   (D) Get different shades of black with which to express a variety of emotions

**Exercise 2** 次の各文が本文の内容に合っていれば T を，合っていなければ F を選びましょう。

1. 【T / F】 The contrast between black and white seems to represent only a limited number of the elements of the universe within a limited framework.

2. 【T / F】 Wang Xizhi and Chu Suiliang left documents relating to their careers which are now recognized as works of art.

3. 【T / F】 All calligraphers have the chance to present their works, because there are many exhibitions held throughout the country.

---

### ◉ 日本語の横書き ◉

日本では古来より中国に倣い、上から下、右行から左行の「縦書き」を採用してきました。日本で「横書き」の概念が生まれたのは、ヨーロッパ言語の影響を受けてのことで、それに倣って左から右へ書くことになりました。寺社の古い扁額や戦前の印刷物などに見られる、一見すると右から左への「横書き」に見える表記は、実は一行に一文字ずつの「縦書き」で、書いた人に「横書き」の認識はなかったはずなのです。

# Writing

**Exercise 1** 日本語に合うように，(  ) 内に適切な語を書き入れましょう。

1. Japanese calligraphy is now (　　　　　) among foreign people.
   （書道は，今では外国人の間で人気です。）

2. People tried to copy the papers, which, (　　　　　) (　　　　　), came to be adopted as a practice method.
   （人々は文書を模倣しようとし，やがてそれが練習方法として確立しました。）

3. Many calligraphy classes are held (　　　　　) Japan.
   （日本中で多くの書道教室が開かれています。）

**Exercise 2** (  ) 内の語を並べ替えて，英文を完成させましょう。

1. Calligraphy in teaching ( has / down / since / in / been / passed / Japan ) the Edo period.
   （教授法としての書道は，日本では江戸時代より受け継がれてきました。）

2. She buys at least ( two / writing-brush / one / years / every ).

3. Copying is ( learning / to / traditional / a / of / how / way ) use the brush.

# Speaking 次の表現を使って，パートナーと話す練習をしましょう。

> A: Thank you for taking me to the museum.
> B: Not at all.
> A: I can send you some flowers, if you like.
> B: That would be kind of you to offer.

**Exercise** 日本語に合うように，英語で表現しましょう。

1. A: Thank you for _____. （パーティーに来る，宿題を手伝う，手紙を書く）
   B: Not at all.

2. A: I can _____, if you like.
   （何か飲み物を持ってくる，パーティーに彼を招く，ハンバーガーを買う）
   B: That would be kind of you to offer.

# Unit 7
## The Mississippi River
### アメリカ最長の河

🔊 **Listening** Warming up  32

◆ 無声化と有声化 ◆

ことばを構成する音には、有声音と無声音があります。後の単語の初めの音に影響されて、前の単語の最後の子音が「音の同化」現象により変化することがあります。

① [t] → [d]（有声化）Get out of here.（ゲダウト）

② [v] → [f]（無声化）"Can you swim?" "Of course I can."（オフコース）

**Exercise 1** CD を聴いて、アメリカのどのような地理の説明か、その名前を日本語で（　）内に書き入れましょう。　　33

A (　　　　　)　　B (　　　　　)　　C (　　　　　)

**Exercise 2** CD を聴いて、最も適切な応答を一つ選びましょう。　　34

1. (A) (B) (C)　　2. (A) (B) (C)　　3. (A) (B) (C)　　4. (A) (B) (C)

**Exercise 3** Opening Conversation を聴いて、下の質問に日本語で答えましょう。　　35

1. Sayaka はアメリカ文学の講義についてどのように話していますか。

..........................................................................................................................

2. David の好きな作家は誰ですか。

..........................................................................................................................

# Reading 英文を読んで，質問に答えましょう。

"What has five eyes and crosses most of the United States?"

This is a classic riddle in the United States. Can you guess what it is? Yes! The answer is the Mississippi River!

The Mississippi River is 2,320 miles (3,730 km) long and flows from Minnesota
5 to the Gulf of Mexico. The river was an important transportation route long before railroads were constructed. Minneapolis is the largest city in Minnesota and is known as the "Mill City." The city developed its lumber and flour milling industries by using hydropower generated from St. Anthony Falls, the highest waterfall on the Mississippi River. There are a series of historic locks and dams, which were used to change the
10 water level so that boats could go down the river.

No author is more closely connected to the Mississippi River than Mark Twain. Born in Missouri, he writes stories set on the river such as *The Adventures of Tom Sawyer* (1876) and *The Adventures of Huckleberry Finn* (1885). You may even have boarded the Mark Twain Riverboat at Tokyo Disneyland.

15 Mark Twain himself hoped to be a river pilot and his pen name came from a term used by captains. The call "mark twain" signified two fathoms. A fathom was a unit of measurement equal to about 1.3 meters and two fathoms referred to the depth of water required for a boat to reach the riverbank. This unit of measurement was especially important for boatmen, who looked forward to anchoring their boats after a
20 long voyage. Unfortunately, Twain had to give up his dream to be a river pilot as trade between the North and the South was prohibited during the American Civil War.

The Mississippi River is one of the United States' transportation arteries and holds a significant role in the country's narrative and culture. Getting a chance to travel along the river is like stepping into a chapter of America's history.

(320 words)

(L. 2) riddle なぞなぞ　(L. 5) the Gulf of Mexico メキシコ湾　(L. 7) lumber 材木　(L. 7) flour milling 製粉
(L. 8) hydropower 水力　(L. 8) waterfall 滝　(L. 9) lock ロック（閘門）　(L. 15) pilot 水先案内人
(L. 16) signify 示す　(L. 16) fathom ファゾム（尋）　(L. 16-17) unit of measurement 測量単位
(L. 19) anchor 船を停泊する　(L. 21) the American Civil War 南北戦争　(L. 22) artery 動脈，幹線
(L. 23) narrative 物語

**Exercise 1** 本文を読んで，下の質問に答えましょう。

1. Where does the Mississippi River run?
   (A) It runs all through the United States, from north to south.
   (B) It runs along the border between the United States and Mexico.
   (C) It runs through almost all of the states in the United States.
   (D) It runs through Minnesota, Missouri, and Mexico.

2. Why is Minneapolis called the "Mill City"?
   (A) It is the biggest city in Minnesota with a population of around one million.
   (B) It is famous for millions of lakes popular with visitors from overseas.
   (C) It transported a lot of mills to other parts of the United States.
   (D) It flourished as a city by running mills for lumber and flour production.

3. What did Mark Twain do?
   (A) He worked on the Mississippi riverboats throughout his life.
   (B) He used the Mississippi River as the setting of some of his stories.
   (C) He fought for the North during the American Civil War.
   (D) He visited Tokyo to design an attraction for Tokyo Disneyland.

**Exercise 2** 次の各文が本文の内容に合っていればTを，合っていなければFを選びましょう。

1. 【T / F】 A legend tells of a five-eyed giant living in the Mississippi River.

2. 【T / F】 Locks and dams at St. Anthony Falls enabled navigation between points upstream and downstream.

3. 【T / F】 Mark Twain was named after his father, who was once a Mississippi River pilot.

---

◎ 『ハックルベリー・フィンの冒険』秘話 ◎

トウェインは従来の作家とは異なり，アメリカ英語で作品を書きました。『ハックルベリー・フィンの冒険』の出版当初，粗野な英語表現や浮浪児ハックと黒人奴隷ジムが物語の中心にあることが批判されます。トウェインは自ら新聞広告を出し，「いやらしい（dirty）」出来事が書いてあるためにマサチューセッツ州で禁書になったと，人々の好奇心をあおり，売上げを伸ばしました。

# Writing

**Exercise 1** 日本語に合うように，（ ）内に適切な語を書き入れましょう。

1. (　　　　　) what?  Ayaka won the first prize in the speech contest!
   （何だと思う？　Ayaka がスピーチコンテストで一等賞をもらったの！）

2. University textbooks use a lot of technical (　　　　　).
   （大学の教科書にはたくさんの専門用語が使われています。）

3. I don't like anybody to (　　　　　) into my room when I am away.
   （出かけている時に，誰かに部屋に入られるのはいやです。）

**Exercise 2** （ ）内の語を並べ替えて，英文を完成させましょう。

1. Jim says that ( Huck / be / friend / than / no / could / braver ).
   （ハック以上に勇敢な友人はいないと，ジムは言っています。）

   ................................................................

2. He wrote the story ( it / before / published / long / he ).

   ................................................................

3. Her fans ( book / forward / new / are / to / her / looking ).

   ................................................................

# Speaking 次の表現を使って，パートナーと話す練習をしましょう。

> A: I was surprised to hear that you got a chance to study in the States!
> B: It was a big surprise to me, too!
> A: I'm happy to see you! It's surprising to me that you came all this way to visit me.
> B: That's nice to hear!

**Exercise** 日本語に合うように，英語で表現しましょう。

1. A: I was surprised _____!
   （そのニュース，パンダの赤ちゃんが生まれたこと，あなたが昇進したこと）

   B: It was a great surprise to me, too.

2. A: It was surprising to me _____.
   （誕生日にプレゼントを贈ってくれたこと，私の兄が結婚したこと，作家が私たちの大学を訪れたこと）

   B: That's nice to hear!

# Unit 8
# Ocean Blue
洞窟ダイビングの人気スポット

## 🎧 Listening  Warming up  💿 37

◆ 連結発音（つながる音）◆
日本語は母音で終わる音節が多く，英語は子音で終わる音節が多くあります。自然なスピードで話すとき，語尾の子音と語頭の母音の組み合わせで音声的につながり，別々の単語が一つの単語のように聞こえることがあります。次の例をみてみましょう。（文中での発音練習については付録⑤ p.71 を参照。）

① run away（ラナウェイ）
② in order to（イノーダトゥ）
③ call again（コーラゲン）
④ turn off（ターノフ）
⑤ take care of（テイケアロブ）

**Exercise 1**　CD を聴いて，どのスポーツの説明か，スポーツ名を日本語で（　）内に書き入れましょう。　💿 38

A (　　　　　　　)　　B (　　　　　　　)　　C (　　　　　　　)

**Exercise 2**　CD を聴いて，最も適切な応答を一つ選びましょう。　💿 39

1. (A) (B) (C)　　2. (A) (B) (C)　　3. (A) (B) (C)　　4. (A) (B) (C)

**Exercise 3**　Opening Conversation を聴いて，下の質問に日本語で答えましょう。　💿 40

1. Kenji は去年の夏，何をしましたか。

2. Kenji と David は今年の夏，何をしようとしていますか。

## Reading 英文を読んで，質問に答えましょう。

　Kenji and his diving instructor, Jennifer, were at the jump-off point. She said, "Now, it's your turn, Kenji. David is down there." Kenji took a deep breath and made a big jump into the water. Jennifer followed him.

　She told the two boys to make their next move while floating. David checked his
5 buoyancy and began to go down under the water. Kenji, however, couldn't do the same. His buoyancy prevented him from swimming down. Actually, he took too much air into his lungs. But when Jennifer put two more weights into Kenji's pockets, he could finally go underwater.

　They were heading for the View Spot where the Inner Pool and the Pacific Ocean
10 meet. Gradually, Kenji began to feel the increasing water pressure on his whole body as he went deeper. It was getting darker and darker. The waves of the water surface were no longer visible. Kenji managed to keep his buoyancy neutral while swimming.

　Jennifer showed the signboard to David and Kenji to stop on the way. "What a fantastic sight this is!" Kenji thought with excitement. The undersea tunnels were giving
15 off beautiful light beams against the dark cave. He found three tunnels—the left one had a shining white light, the middle a glimmering purple light, and the right a flickering yellow light.

　Passing through the middle tunnel, they finally got to the View Spot, where a wide variety of tropical fish were gathered. David exclaimed, "Amazing! This really is an
20 ocean paradise." Jennifer said, "No fish feeding. We have to preserve the balance of the ocean environment. It is essential for fish to stay on a natural diet so that they can get the nutrients they need."

(283 words)

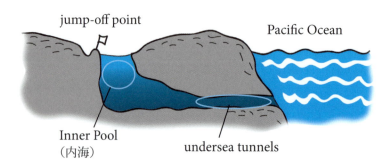

|  |  |  |  |  |
|---|---|---|---|---|
| (L. 4) float 浮かぶ | (L. 5) buoyancy 浮力 | (L. 7) lung 肺 | (L. 7) weight 重り | (L. 13) signboard 水中記録板 |
| (L. 14) fantastic 素晴らしい | (L. 14-15) give off 光を放つ | (L. 16) glimmer ちらちら輝く | | |
| (L. 16) flicker 光がちらつく | (L. 22) nutrients 栄養分 | | | |

**Exercise 1**  本文を読んで，下の質問に答えましょう。

1. Who jumped into the ocean first?
   (A) Kenji
   (B) David
   (C) Jennifer
   (D) Kenji and Jennifer jumped into the ocean first together.

2. What did Jennifer do for Kenji while he was floating?
   (A) She asked Kenji to take a deep breath.
   (B) She asked David to pull Kenji down.
   (C) She dropped more weights into Kenji's pockets.
   (D) She asked David to give some weights to Kenji.

3. What did Kenji notice as he went deeper?
   (A) A strange thing was happening to his body.
   (B) The water pressure was increasing.
   (C) He could not see the waves on the surface anymore.
   (D) His training for maintaining a neutral buoyancy did not help him.

**Exercise 2**  次の各文が本文の内容に合っていればTを，合っていなければFを選びましょう。

1. 【T / F】 The "jump-off point" is the place at which Kenji jumped into the ocean.

2. 【T / F】 Kenji got excited when he saw the beautiful tropical fish at the "View Spot."

3. 【T / F】 Jennifer advised Kenji and David not to feed the fish for health and environmental reasons.

---

## 🔵 スキューバ・ダイビング 🔵

スキューバ・ダイビングは，中性浮力 "neutral buoyancy"（浮きも沈みもしない状態）を常に保つことが重要です。深さによる浮力の変化に応じて，ジャケット内の空気量を調節する必要があるため，頭脳的なスポーツだと言われています。また，ダイビング中は，二人一組で行動するバディシステムと呼ばれる方式で行動します。

# Writing

**Exercise 1** 日本語に合うように，（　）内に適切な語を書き入れましょう。

1. Scuba diving is a popular marine sport (　　　　) young people.
   （スキューバダイビングは若者に人気のある海のスポーツです。）

2. The storm (　　　　) us from (　　　　) a diving trip to Okinawa.
   （嵐のために私たちは沖縄にダイビング旅行に行けませんでした。）

3. When she reached the undersea tunnels, she exclaimed, "(　　　　) (　　　　) beautiful sight this is!"
   （海底のトンネルに到着した時，彼女は「なんて美しい景色だろう！」と叫びました。）

**Exercise 2** （　）内の語を並べ替えて，英文を完成させましょう。

1. There ( mountains / at / are / and / bottom / the / some / tunnels ) of the ocean.
   （海の底に山やトンネルがあります。）

2. It is important ( follow / divers / for / rules / to / scuba ) in the ocean.

3. You must try ( as / ocean / found / leave / environment / the / you / to / it ).

# Speaking 次の表現を使って，パートナーと話す練習をしましょう。

> A: Why don't you join the sightseeing tour?
> B: That sounds nice. I will.
> A: How about going for a drive this weekend?
> B: I'm sorry. I already have another engagement.

**Exercise** 日本語に合うように，英語で表現しましょう。

1. A: Why don't you ＿＿＿＿＿＿＿＿?
   （パーティーに参加する，クラブのミーティングに行く，東京ディズニーランドに行く）
   B: That sounds nice. I will.

2. A: How about ＿＿＿＿＿＿＿＿?
   （中国料理を食べる，名古屋駅で会う，ユニバーサル・スタジオ・ジャパンに行く）
   B: I'm sorry. I already have another engagement.

# Unit 9
# Studying Abroad
留学する前に考えておくべきことは

## 🎧 Listening   Warming up                  42

◆ 英語のリズム ◆

英語では強く発音される部分が等間隔で現れます。「弱・強・弱・強……」のようなリズムに乗って，一定の間隔で発音練習しましょう。
（小さい●が弱，大きい●が強，★は一番強調する部分を表します。）

　　●●・●・●●・・　●★
① A cat with a cap is on the mat.

　　●★　●●・●・●・
② She sells seashells by the seashore.

**Exercise 1**　CD を聴いて，何の説明か，その名前を日本語で（　）内に書き入れましょう。　　43

A (　　　　　　　)　　B (　　　　　　　　)　　C (　　　　　　　　)

**Exercise 2**　CD を聴いて，最も適切な応答を一つ選びましょう。　　44

1. (A) (B) (C)　　2. (A) (B) (C)　　3. (A) (B) (C)　　4. (A) (B) (C)

**Exercise 3**　Opening Conversation を聴いて，下の質問に日本語で答えましょう。　　45

1. Sayaka は，David が話しかける前に何をしていましたか。

　　………………………………………………………………………………………………

2. 留学について Sayaka の相談に乗ってくれそうなのは誰ですか。

　　………………………………………………………………………………………………

# Reading 英文を読んで，質問に答えましょう。

If you are a student majoring in English or another foreign language, then you have probably thought about studying abroad. Immersing yourself in another culture is much more than simply improving your language abilities. It is also about finding your independence in an environment entirely different from your own. It is an undertaking that will test your character.

An important question to ask yourself is, what do you want to gain from this experience? It is essential that you make your goals clear from the beginning because you will have to make some critical choices.

Two of the major decisions you will have to make is where and what to study. Make sure to check out a variety of universities and the courses they offer international students. Some students may want to focus on intensive language training while others may want to study other subjects, such as history or business, in a foreign language. There might also be programs that allow you to gain valuable work experience while you study.

Unfortunately, studying abroad costs a lot of money. Many students work multiple part-time jobs so that they can raise the necessary funds, but keep in mind that there are scholarships and other financial aid options available. Remember to consult the office in charge of international study programs at your university.

As much as people love to highlight the positive aspects of studying abroad, the reality is that you will be facing all sorts of problems and difficulties, from jet lag to culture shock. However, studying abroad will ultimately give you a broader and more globalized perspective. It is an opportunity to challenge the perceptions that you have about yourself and the world.

(282 words)

(L. 2) immerse 身を置く　　(L. 4) undertaking 仕事　　(L. 8) critical 重大な　　(L. 11) intensive 集中的な
(L. 15) multiple 多数の　　(L. 17) scholarship 奨学金　　(L. 17) option 選択　　(L. 19) highlight 強調する
(L. 20) jet lag 時差ボケ　　(L. 21) ultimately 結局　　(L. 22) perspective 見方　　(L. 22) perception 認識

**Exercise 1** 本文を読んで，下の質問に答えましょう。

1. Which of the following sentences is true?
   (A) The most important thing about studying abroad is learning a foreign language.
   (B) Studying abroad is only for students who are learning English.
   (C) Living in a different cultural environment is a test of character.
   (D) Studying abroad is something everyone should do.

2. According to the text, if you are thinking about going abroad to study, one question that you need to ask yourself is:
   (A) Which country has a culture similar to your own?
   (B) How can I easily make friends?
   (C) What is it that I want to get out of the whole experience?
   (D) How can I make sure that my language skills are perfect?

3. Which of the following might be encountered when studying abroad?
   (A) Culture shock
   (B) Cross-cultural communication issues
   (C) Jet-lag
   (D) All of the above

**Exercise 2** 次の各文が本文の内容に合っていればTを，合っていなければFを選びましょう。

1. 【T / F】 Studying abroad is all about improving your language skills.
2. 【T / F】 You have to work more than one part-time job to raise money for studying abroad.
3. 【T / F】 Studying abroad can be a life-changing experience but it comes with difficulties and challenges.

---

### ◎ カルチャーショック ◎

海外で過ごしたことのある人は，何らかのカルチャーショックを経験したことがあるでしょう。カルチャーショックとは，馴染みのない文化に触れた時に起こる感情的・精神的・身体的な反応のことです。頭痛がしたり，家が恋しくなったり，疲れていらだったり，相手の価値観や習慣に対して過剰に批判的になったりします。カルチャーショックを克服するのは簡単ではありませんが，誰もが経験する自然な反応だということも覚えておくべきです。

# Writing

**Exercise 1** 日本語に合うように，（ ）内に適切な語を書き入れましょう。

1. Studying abroad is a chance to find your (　　　　) in a different culture.
   （留学は，違った文化の中で自立を試みる機会です。）

2. You need to think and decide on your (　　　　) from the beginning.
   （あなたは当初から目的について考え，決定する必要があります。）

3. Don't forget to check what financial aid programs are (　　　　) to you.
   （どんな資金援助が受けられるのか確認するのを忘れてはいけません。）

**Exercise 2** （ ）内の語を並べ替えて，英文を完成させましょう。

1. Where and what to study are two ( you / that / to / questions / answer / yourself / for / need ).
   （どこで何を勉強するかは，自ら答えを出さなければならない2つの課題です。）

   ....................................................................................................................................

2. Some study abroad programs ( on / focus / only / might ) intensive language training.

   ....................................................................................................................................

3. Many students work multiple part-time jobs ( save / order / money / for / in / abroad / studying / to ).

   ....................................................................................................................................

# Speaking 次の表現を使って，パートナーと話す練習をしましょう。

> A: Would you know how I can learn more about study abroad programs?
> B: Maybe you can ask Professor Iyoda.
> A: What can I do to get more exercise?
> B: Maybe you could try walking for at least 30 minutes every day.

**Exercise** 日本語に合うように，英語で表現しましょう。

1. A: What can I do to improve my English?
   B: Maybe you could try _____ in English.　（映画を観る，音楽を聴く，本を読む）

2. A: Who can I ask about studying abroad?
   B: Maybe you could ask your _____.　（クラスメイト，先生，アドバイザー）

# Unit 10
# The Northern Lights
カナダのオーロラ観光

## 🔊 Listening　Warming up　 47

◆ イントネーション ◆

音の高低の変化をイントネーションと言います。疑問文を全て上げ調子で言っていませんか？確かに，Yes–No 疑問文は上げ調子になりますが，What や How などの疑問詞疑問文は，基本的に下げ調子で言うのが一般的です。また，イントネーションには大きく分けて 3 種類のパターンがあります。付録④（p.70）で詳しく解説します。"Yes" は，下げ調子（だんだんと下げる），上げ調子（だんだんと上げる），下げてから上げる調子で次のような意味の違いがあります。表記のイメージと合わせて見てみましょう。

はい。　　Yes　　　　はい？　Yes　　　　はい…　Yes
（肯定的な返事）　　（疑問のある返事）　　（含みのある返事）

**Exercise 1**　CD を聴いて，カナダのどのような風物の説明か，その名前を日本語で（ ）内に書き入れましょう。　48

A (　　　　　　　)　　B (　　　　　　　)　　C (　　　　　　　)

**Exercise 2**　CD を聴いて，最も適切な応答を一つ選びましょう。　49

1. (A) (B) (C)　　2. (A) (B) (C)　　3. (A) (B) (C)　　4. (A) (B) (C)

**Exercise 3**　Opening Conversation を聴いて，下の質問に日本語で答えましょう。　50

1. Sayaka はどこに留学することを考えていますか。

2. オーロラを見られる場所はカナダのどこですか。

## Reading 英文を読んで，質問に答えましょう。

　There are a lot of beautiful places in Canada. Along with major cities like Vancouver, Toronto, Ottawa, Quebec City, and Montreal, Japanese tourists like to visit places filled with natural splendor and enjoy the magnificent scenery. Among them are Niagara Falls, Prince Edward Island, Banff, and Whistler.

5　Yellowknife is also a popular destination for Japanese tourists. It is the capital city of the Northwest Territories, which is located close to the edge of the Arctic Circle. The main thing attracting tourists is that they might get to see aurora borealis, more commonly known as the northern lights. Traveling to Yellowknife reached its peak in the early 2000s, but seeing the northern lights continues to be a dream shared by many
10 people from Japan and other countries.

　The northern lights are natural phenomena that have long fascinated people. The lights are mostly green but also come in other colors such as red, pink, blue, and violet. The lights can be faint or bright. They can hang like ribbons in the sky or move dynamically, depending on the sun, the earth's magnetic field, the location from which
15 they are viewed, the time, and the season.

　Yellowknife has a multi-ethnic population and is the traditional home of the First Nations people called Dene. Some Dene people believe that those who have passed away walk up the stairs of the northern lights to join their ancestors in heaven. Some of them also think that they can bring the lights down to the ground and make them dance
20 by whistling and rubbing their fingernails. Conversely, in Nunavut, some believe that, when they are scared, they can make the lights go away by rubbing their fingernails. The beliefs and stories told about the northern lights reflect the lights' beauty, mystery, and ability to inspire people.

(299 words)

(L. 3) splendor みごとさ　(L. 6) the Northwest Territories 北西準州　(L. 6) the Arctic Circle 北極圏
(L. 7, 8) aurora borealis / the northern lights オーロラ　(L. 11) phenomenon 現象　(L. 11) fascinate 魅了する
(L. 14) dynamically 力強く　(L. 14) the magnetic field 磁場　(L. 16) multi-ethnic 多民族の
(L. 16-17) the First Nations people カナダ先住民　(L. 17) Dene デネ（族）　(L. 20) whistle 口笛を鳴らす
(L. 20) rub こする　(L. 20) fingernail 爪　(L. 20) conversely 反対に　(L. 20) Nunavut ヌナヴト準州

**Exercise 1** 本文を読んで，下の質問に答えましょう。

1. Why is Yellowknife popular among Japanese tourists?
   (A) It is the largest city in the Northwest Territories.
   (B) It is the only city within the Arctic Circle.
   (C) They might be able to see the northern lights if they go there.
   (D) They feel that it is a safe and easy location to travel to.

2. What are the "northern lights"?
   (A) They are special lights invented in the Northwest Territories.
   (B) They are natural light displays visible only from the Northwest Territories.
   (C) They are natural phenomena commonly found all over Canada.
   (D) They are colorful lights that nature produces in northern regions.

3. What do some Dene people believe?
   (A) The northern lights are stairs to heaven.
   (B) The northern lights are their descendants.
   (C) The northern lights are fingers from heaven.
   (D) The northern lights are difficult to control.

**Exercise 2** 次の各文が本文の内容に合っていればTを，合っていなければFを選びましょう。

1. 【T / F】 Canada's magnificent scenery is one of the reasons why so many Japanese tourists travel to Canada.

2. 【T / F】 The appearance of the northern lights varies according to different natural conditions.

3. 【T / F】 There are few beliefs and stories told about the northern lights by the First Nations people.

---

### 🔵 イエローナイフ 🔵

カナダには，10の州と3つの準州があります。北西準州（ノースウェスト準州），ユーコン準州，ヌナヴト準州はいずれもカナダ北部に位置し，先住民人口を多く抱えています。北西準州は，金やダイヤモンド，ウラン等の鉱業で栄え，準州都のイエローナイフは，デネ語族のひとつであるドグリブ語で，「ソンバケ」（金のある場所：the money place）と呼ばれています。

## Writing

**Exercise 1** 日本語に合うように，（ ）内に適切な語を書き入れましょう。

1. It is difficult to find accommodation at the (　　　　　) of the holiday season.
   （休暇シーズンの最盛期には，宿泊施設を見つけるのは難しいです。）

2. Hazuki (　　　　　) a house with three other students in Canada.
   （Hazuki は，カナダで他の学生 3 人と共同で家を借りました。）

3. (　　　　　), younger people started to choose Canada as a travel destination.
   （反対に，若い人たちが旅先にカナダを選ぶようになりました。）

**Exercise 2** （ ）内の語を並べ替えて，英文を完成させましょう。

1. Canada ( of / with / policy / has / multiculturalism / a / along / adopted ) many other countries.
   （他の多くの国々と同様に，カナダは多文化主義政策を取っています。）

2. I read a lot of animal stories in my childhood; ( are / by / among / works / them ) the Canadian author E. T. Seaton.

3. Canada has two official languages; ( speak / those / called / who / French / are / in ) Francophones.

## Speaking 次の表現を使って，パートナーと話す練習をしましょう。

> A: How far is it?
> B: It's a ten-minute walk from the university.
> A: How long will it take to get there?
> B: It will take about two hours by train.

**Exercise** 日本語に合うように，英語で表現しましょう。

1. A: How far is it?
   B: It's _____. （駅から約 2 キロ，レストランから歩いて 3 分，郵便局から車で約 5 分）

2. A: How long will it take to get there?
   B: It will take _____. （ほんの 10 分，バスで 1 時間，飛行機で 7 時間）

# Unit 11
## The Sound of the Saxophone
サキソフォンの魅力的な音色

### 🔊 Listening  Warming up  52

◆ 紛らわしい音 ◆

日本語に存在しない音や，日本語では区別されない音は聞き取りも発音も難しいです。例えば，英語には上歯と下唇を使って出す [f] や [v] の音があります。その他に，[l] と [r] や [θ] と [s] などの区別が間違いやすいので気を付けましょう。

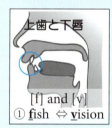

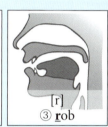

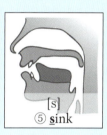

**Exercise 1**　CD を聴いて，どの楽器の説明か，その楽器の名前を日本語で（　）内に書き入れましょう。　53

A (　　　　　　)　　B (　　　　　　)　　C (　　　　　　)

**Exercise 2**　CD を聴いて，最も適切な応答を一つ選びましょう。 54

1. (A) (B) (C)　　2. (A) (B) (C)　　3. (A) (B) (C)　　4. (A) (B) (C)

**Exercise 3**　Opening Conversation を聴いて，下の質問に日本語で答えましょう。 55

1. コンサートで演奏される曲目のジャンルは何ですか。

　

2. コンサート会場は Nadia 音楽大学のどこですか。

## Reading 英文を読んで，質問に答えましょう。

　There are no civilizations or cultures without musical instruments. In modern times, whether it's through popular songs or classical music, we enjoy the beautiful sounds created by musical instruments. To produce complex and dynamic music, a symphony orchestra is composed of strings, brass, and percussion. Saxophones, however, are rarely included in symphony orchestras.

　The saxophone is a relatively new instrument invented by Adolphe Sax in the 1840s. This instrument is becoming increasingly popular among people of all ages. It is said that the sound quality of the saxophone is mild and similar to the human voice. Thus, saxophone instructors often advise their learners to "play as if you are singing." It does not take a beginner long to find pleasure in playing the instrument.

　In the case of the flute, sound is created by human breath passing through brass. Unlike the flute, the saxophone needs a reed to make music. Master saxophonists develop sophisticated techniques and are able to vibrate their reeds in order to manipulate the sound they make. From classical to jazz, saxophonists are thus able to adjust to different musical genres.

　As exciting as a solo performance by a saxophonist is, ensembles with more than one saxophone combined with other instruments sound even more incredible. In a jazz band, while other players provide accompaniment on piano, bass guitar, and drums, the saxophonists are able to blend their sound with the other musicians' in order to create beautiful harmonies.

　While visiting London, I came upon a street musician playing jazz on the saxophone. I could sense the power of the saxophone just by looking at his face. The touching sound of the saxophone makes a unique connection with the human spirit because of its power to stimulate even the deepest parts of one's soul.

(296 words)

(L. 1) musical instrument 楽器　(L. 3) complex 複雑な　(L. 3-4) symphony orchestra 交響楽団
(L. 6) Adolphe Sax アドルフ・サックス（楽器製作者）　(L. 7) increasingly ますます　(L. 12) reed リード
(L. 13) sophisticated 洗練された　(L. 13) vibrate 振動させる　(L. 14) manipulate 巧みに操る
(L. 15) genre ジャンル　(L. 16) solo 独奏　(L. 16) ensemble アンサンブル　(L. 17) incredible すばらしい
(L. 18) accompaniment 伴奏　(L. 22) touching 感動的な　(L. 24) stimulate 刺激する　(L. 24) soul 魂

**Exercise 1**  本文を読んで，下の質問に答えましょう。

1. Which of these statements is true about a symphony orchestra?
   (A) It consists of just one type of instrument.
   (B) The instruments are grouped together according to type.
   (C) It can produce all kinds of music except classical music.
   (D) The saxophone is a most popular instrument in an orchestra.

2. How do skilled saxophonists vary their sound?
   (A) They blow into their saxophones without a reed.
   (B) They copy other musicians' techniques.
   (C) They try to vibrate their reeds.
   (D) They use more expensive saxophones.

3. What do saxophone players in a jazz band do to entertain the audience?
   (A) They play solo, one instrument at a time.
   (B) They ignore the other instrumentalists in the band.
   (C) They swap instruments and play piano, bass guitar, and drums.
   (D) They produce beautiful harmonies with the other instruments.

**Exercise 2**  次の各文が本文の内容に合っていればTを，合っていなければFを選びましょう。

1. 【T / F】 A symphony orchestra always includes the saxophone as one of its major instruments.

2. 【T / F】 The sound quality of the saxophone is said to resemble the human voice.

3. 【T / F】 The sound of the saxophone is uplifting and entertaining.

(uplift: 気持ちを高揚させる)

---

### ● サックスとジャズ ●

サックスは，ジャズの演奏でよく使われる楽器の一つです。透き通った美しい音色に魅せられている人も数多くいることでしょう。ジャズには即興でアレンジされたオリジナル曲を味わえる醍醐味があります。なじみのあるクラシック曲もテンポやリズムを変えて，スイング風になると，まるで違う別世界の曲のように感じられます。

# Writing

**Exercise 1** 日本語に合うように，（ ）内に適切な語を書き入れましょう。

1. The saxophone is a new musical instrument (　　　　　) in the 19th century.
   （サキソフォンは 19 世紀に発明された新しい楽器です。）

2. This musical instrument is becoming (　　　　　) popular among young people.
   （この楽器は，若者の間でますます人気が出てきています。）

3. (　　　　　) language, music can convey messages to people from different cultural backgrounds.
   （言語とは違って，音楽は異なる文化圏の人たちにメッセージを伝えることができます。）

**Exercise 2** （ ）内の語を並べ替えて，英文を完成させましょう。

1. You ( concert / the / get / at / tickets / can / saxophone ) the box office.
   （サキソフォンコンサートのチケットを切符売り場で買うことができます。）

   ..........................................................................................................

2. This current ( is / piece / exciting / of / as / jazz ) as that one.

   ..........................................................................................................

3. We listened ( with / violinist / in / the / harmony / to / playing / perfect ) the pianist.

   ..........................................................................................................

# 💬 Speaking 次の表現を使って，パートナーと話す練習をしましょう。

> A: Will you carry this bag for me?　　A: I would like you to come to the party.
> B: OK. No problem.　　　　　　　　　B: Sure. With pleasure.

**Exercise** 日本語に合うように，英語で表現しましょう。

1. A: Will you _____?
   （窓を開ける，電気を消す，あなたのメールアドレスを私に教える）
   B: OK. No problem.

2. A: I would like you to _____.
   （学園祭に参加する，あなたのノートを私に貸す，私のプレゼンテーションを手伝う）
   B: Sure. With pleasure.

# Unit 12
# Communication Tips
良好な人間関係を築くには

## 🎧 Listening  Warming up   57

◆ 半母音 ◆

英語の「半母音」には，[w]と[j]の2つがあります。日本語のワ行とヤ行に相当します。[w]は唇を突き出して「ゥア」，[j]は「イゥ」と発音します。間違いやすいですが，それぞれ「ウ」や「イ」ではありません。例えば，yeast は <u>イースト</u> ではなく，<u>イィー</u> ストと発音します。woman の [w] は唇を丸めて突き出して発音します。

[j]　① **y**east　② **y**acht　③ **y**ellow

[w]　④ **w**ool　⑤ **w**ater　⑥ **w**ish

**Exercise 1** CD を聴いて，何の説明か，その名前を日本語で（　）内に書き入れましょう。　58

A (　　　　　)　　B (　　　　　)　　C (　　　　　)

**Exercise 2** CD を聴いて，最も適切な応答を一つ選びましょう。　59

1. (A) (B) (C)　　2. (A) (B) (C)　　3. (A) (B) (C)　　4. (A) (B) (C)

**Exercise 3** Opening Conversation を聴いて，下の質問に日本語で答えましょう。　60

1. Sayaka が話しかけた時に Miyabi は何をしていましたか。

   ......................................................................................................................

2. David の Sayaka へのアドバイスは何でしたか。

   ......................................................................................................................

**Reading** 英文を読んで，質問に答えましょう。

Being able to communicate clearly and effectively is not a skill that everyone has. Communication skills are essential tools in almost every aspect of life—whether you are looking for a job, asking someone for a favor, or making a new friend. One form of communication that perhaps deserves special attention is that of personal interaction. When it comes to getting your message across, it is not simply about what you say, but how you say it. As crucial as having a firm grasp of vocabulary and grammar is, it is equally important to master the art of communicating through gestures and facial expressions in order to be an engaging communicator.

The first thing to remember is to make eye contact. This is not only a mark of confidence but also gives the impression that you intend to understand what the other person has to say.

The second point to keep in mind is paying attention to your body language. Are your arms folded across your chest? Are you drumming your fingers on the table? These are things people tend to do when they are defensive, impatient, or nervous. When people get nervous, there is a need for that nervous energy to escape. Try and find out what you tend to do when you are nervous or uncomfortable. Then you can think of appropriate solutions and learn to relax more. Subtle motions such as nodding your head, leaning forward slightly, and smiling will bring an air of positivity into your conversation.

Finally, make sure to respect the people with whom you are speaking. Good manners are the best way to show them that you value their time and presence.

(279 words)

(L. 4) personal interaction 対人相互作用　(L. 6) crucial 重要な　(L. 6) grasp 把握　(L. 6) vocabulary 語彙
(L. 7) art こつ　(L. 7-8) facial expression 顔の表情　(L. 13) fold 腕を組む　(L. 13) chest 胸
(L. 13) drum（太鼓のように）鳴らす　(L. 14) defensive 防御的な　(L. 14) impatient イライラする
(L. 14) nervous 緊張した　(L. 17) subtle かすかな

**Exercise 1**　本文を読んで，下の質問に答えましょう。

1. Which of the following statements about communication is true?
   (A) Perfect grammar is always the most important thing.
   (B) Eye contact is extremely important.
   (C) If you are feeling nervous, just keep quiet.
   (D) Drumming your fingers on the table is a sign that you are listening.

2. Making eye contact …
   (A) can show that you have confidence.
   (B) is a sign that you are truly listening.
   (C) is a signal that you are trying to understand what your partner is saying.
   (D) All of the above

3. Which of the following is NOT true?
   (A) Respecting the people around you is a basic rule of effective communication.
   (B) Communication skills are essential to everyday life.
   (C) Improving communication skills is important only for professionals.
   (D) Mastery of vocabulary and grammar is important but is not the most important factor in communication.

**Exercise 2**　次の各文が本文の内容に合っていれば T を，合っていなければ F を選びましょう。

1. 【T / F】 It is not only what you say that is important, but also the way you express your thoughts.

2. 【T / F】 Folding your arms across your chest is a sign of openness and interest.

3. 【T / F】 Nodding your head while you are listening can help create a relaxed and positive atmosphere.

### 🔵 人とのコミュニケーション 🔵

他の人と交流する時はいつでも，前向きでなごやかな姿勢で臨めば，コミュニケーションが一層スムーズになる傾向があります。こうするための最も効果的な方法は，良いマナーを実践することです。良いマナーとは敬意を払っているということを相手に示すことです。微笑んだり，「どうぞ」や「ありがとう」と言う習慣を身につけるなど，ちょっとしたことで，人とのコミュニケーションが自信に満ちて，より円滑なものになるでしょう。

# Writing

**Exercise 1** 日本語に合うように，（　）内に適切な語を書き入れましょう。

1. Making eye contact without being nervous takes (　　　　　).
   (イライラしないでアイコンタクトを取るためには，練習が必要です。)

2. What do you do to relax (　　　　　) you are nervous?
   (あなたが緊張している時，落ち着くために何をしますか。)

3. Instagram is a useful communication app but it (　　　　　) also be a distraction (　　　　　) your studies.
   (インスタグラムは役に立つコミュニケーションアプリですが，同時に勉強の妨げになる可能性があります。)

**Exercise 2** （　）内の語を並べ替えて，英文を完成させましょう。

1. Effective communicators have mastered ( gestures / use / the / facial / expressions / and / of ).
   (コミュニケーションが得意な人は身振りや顔の表情を巧みに利用しています。)

   ..............................................................................................................................

2. Do you fold your arms ( nervous / are / you / when )?

   ..............................................................................................................................

3. Make sure to show respect for ( you / speaking / are / with / people / the ).

   ..............................................................................................................................

## Speaking　次の表現を使って，パートナーと話す練習をしましょう。

> A: What did you think of the movie we saw yesterday?
> B: I thought it was awesome!
> A: What did you think of our reading assignment?
> B: I felt like it was too easy.

**Exercise** 日本語に合うように，英語で表現しましょう。

1. A: What did you think of the exam yesterday?
   B: I thought it was _____.　(難しかった，簡単だった，複雑だった)

2. A: What did you think of the lecture yesterday?
   B: I felt that it was _____.　(面白かった，わかりやすかった，少し難しかった)

# Unit 13
# Seasonal Festivals (*Sekku*)
9月9日は菊のお節句

## 🎧 Listening  Warming up  62

◆ 英語らしい響き（日本語と英語の違い）◆

日本語には「あいうえお」の5つの母音しかありませんが，英語には15個程あります（付録① p.67 参照）。口の開き具合，舌の位置，唇の丸め具合の3点が重要です。例えば，cat と cut は微妙に響きが異なります。カタカナに惑わされないようにしましょう。

| | | | |
|---|---|---|---|
| 「ア」に似て聞こえる音 | ① cat | ⇔ | cut |
| 「イ」に似て聞こえる音 | ② ship | ⇔ | sheep |
| 「ウ」に似て聞こえる音 | ③ pool | ⇔ | pull |
| 「エ」に似て聞こえる音 | ④ pet | ⇔ | pit |
| 「オ」に似て聞こえる音 | ⑤ mop | ⇔ | map |

**Exercise 1**　CD を聴いて，何の説明か，その名前を日本語で（　）内に書き入れましょう。　63

A (　　　　　)　　B (　　　　　)　　C (　　　　　)

**Exercise 2**　CD を聴いて，最も適切な応答を一つ選びましょう。　64

1. (A) (B) (C)　　2. (A) (B) (C)　　3. (A) (B) (C)　　4. (A) (B) (C)

**Exercise 3**　Opening Conversation を聴いて，下の質問に日本語で答えましょう。　65

1. Mary が出演する劇はどのような内容ですか。

　

2. 劇はどこで上演されますか。

## Reading 英文を読んで，質問に答えましょう。

Although there are four separate seasons throughout the temperate zone, no other culture places more importance on the seasons than Japan. Traditional imperial events were always carried out according to the seasons. The five seasonal festivals, or *sekku*, are among such occasions.

Each seasonal festival has a plant associated with it. The first festival of the New Year is associated with seven herbs which are eaten in rice porridge on the seventh day. The Girls' Festival on March 3 features peach blossoms. A collection of dolls is displayed in the homes of families with young girls. The Boys' Festival, featuring iris flowers, marks the beginning of summer on the lunar calendar. On May 5, families with boys raise colorful carp-shaped streamers and display suits of armor and helmets. The Star Festival, which features bamboo grass, is celebrated on the seventh of July. Stars could be seen more clearly on this day in the past when, according to the old calendar, July 7 fell one month later during the summer.

The last of the five festivals is presently the least well-known. During the Chrysanthemum Festival held on September 9, dolls made of fresh chrysanthemum flowers of various colors used to be displayed. Bunches of chrysanthemum flowers and leaves were shaped into life-size dolls and arranged to portray famous characters from history, folk tales, or TV shows. It was customary to decorate houses with chrysanthemum flowers to scare away evil spirits in the hope of a long life.

The Japanese people have always incorporated the seasons into their daily lives. Many words and phrases associated with the seasons are found in the Japanese language. Taking in the various seasonal aspects of nature may be a good example of the cultural richness of Japan.

(291 words)

(L. 1) temperate zone 温帯　(L. 2) imperial 宮中の　(L. 4) occasion 行事，儀式
(L. 5) associate with ... 〜と関連付ける　(L. 6) rice porridge 粥　(L. 7) blossom 花　(L. 8) iris 菖蒲
(L. 9) lunar calendar 太陰暦，旧暦　(L. 10) streamer 吹き流し　(L. 10) suit of armor 鎧　(L. 10) helmet 兜
(L. 11) bamboo grass 笹　(L. 15) chrysanthemum 菊　(L. 17) life-size 等身大の
(L. 18) be customary to ... 〜する習慣がある

**Exercise 1** 本文を読んで，下の質問に答えましょう。

1. Why could stars be seen more clearly on July 7 in the past?
   (A) A collection of dolls were displayed beautifully.
   (B) Beautiful streamers and warrior's equipment were displayed.
   (C) The sky was clear during the summer months.
   (D) The event was associated with bamboo grass.

2. Which is NOT true about the fifth seasonal festival?
   (A) People used to display dolls made of fake chrysanthemum flowers.
   (B) Famous people were portrayed using bunches of flowers and leaves.
   (C) The Chrysanthemum Festival is not widely known even among Japanese people.
   (D) The festival was held on the ninth day of September.

3. Why did people decorate their houses with chrysanthemum flowers?
   (A) To match the dolls made of chrysanthemum flowers inside their houses.
   (B) The chrysanthemum flowers are associated with the season.
   (C) The older calendar was used to show the date of the festival.
   (D) It was believed that chrysanthemum flowers frightened away the evil.

**Exercise 2** 次の各文が本文の内容に合っていればTを，合っていなければFを選びましょう。

1. 【T / F】 All areas in the temperate zone have four distinct seasons, but no other culture places as much emphasis on the seasons as Japan.
2. 【T / F】 On the third day of March, a set of dolls is put out on display in the houses of families with little girls.
3. 【T / F】 Japanese people have only recently started to incorporate the seasons into their everyday lives.

○ 五節句の日付 ○

節句は1月7日の「人日(じんじつ)」を除き，奇数が重なる日に行われます。これは，奇数を陽，偶数を陰とする陰陽道に基づいています。3月3日が「上巳(じょうし)」，5月5日が「端午(たんご)」，7月7日が「七夕(たなばた)」，9月9日が「重陽(ちょうよう)」です。一桁奇数の中では9がいちばん大きいので，最も陽の力が強いとされ，それが重なるため，重陽の節句がいちばんの慶日なのです。

# Writing

**Exercise 1** 日本語に合うように，（ ）内に適切な語を書き入れましょう。

1. Some festivals are held (　　　　) (　　　　) the older calendar.
   （祭事の中には，旧暦に従って行われるものもあります。）

2. The New Year (　　　　) the beginning of spring on the lunar calendar.
   （太陰暦では，新年が春の始まりを示します。）

3. Seasons (　　　　) (　　　　) into Japanese dishes.
   （和食には，季節感が取り入れられます。）

**Exercise 2** （ ）内の語を並べ替えて，英文を完成させましょう。

1. Pumpkins are ( the / of / December / on / 22nd / eaten / often ).
   （12月22日には，カボチャがよく食べられます。）
   ................................................................

2. It was ( paper / float / customary / dolls / to ) in rivers to dispose of evil.
   ................................................................

3. Many ( associated / found / seasons / with / in / poems / are ) Japanese literature.
   ................................................................

# Speaking 次の表現を使って，パートナーと話す練習をしましょう。

> A: What's new with you?
> B: Well, I'm giving a presentation next week.
> A: Could you tell me how much the textbook is?
> B: Sure.

**Exercise** 日本語に合うように，英語で表現しましょう。

1. A: What's new with you?
   B: Well, I'm _____. （来年留学する，劇場で歌う，写真を展示する）

2. A: Could you tell me _____?
   （授業がどのくらいの長さか，どこへ行くべきか，何が最善か）
   B: Sure.

# Unit 14
# Electric Cars
環境にやさしい車

## 🎧 Listening  Warming up  💿 67

◆ 数字の聞き取り ◆
大きな数字の表現の仕方に慣れましょう。ネイティブの発音を聴いて，どのように音が変化するか確認してみましょう。また，日付や金額の表現は，特殊な読み方をする場合もあるので，注意しましょう。

million 100万　　billion 10億　　trillion 1兆
区切り方（例）1,350,000: one million, three hundred and fifty thousand

① July 4（日付）　　② in 2018（西暦）　　③ $10.50（金額）

**Exercise 1**　CDを聴いて，何の説明か，その名前を日本語で（　）内に書き入れましょう。　💿 68

A (　　　　　　　)　　B (　　　　　　　)　　C (　　　　　　　)

**Exercise 2**　CDを聴いて，最も適切な応答を一つ選びましょう。　💿 69

1. (A) (B) (C)　　2. (A) (B) (C)　　3. (A) (B) (C)　　4. (A) (B) (C)

**Exercise 3**　Opening Conversationを聴いて，下の質問に日本語で答えましょう。　💿 70

1. Kenjiの父親は何を家に取り付けることを決めましたか。

　　..................................................................................................................................

2. Davidは電気の使用で何が起こると言っていますか。

　　..................................................................................................................................

## Reading 英文を読んで，質問に答えましょう。

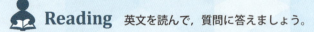

With the growing environmental threat posed by climate change, demand for electric cars is expected to increase. Electric cars have some excellent qualities which distinguish them from conventional cars. The most significant of these qualities is the so-called "Zero Emission Feature," which means that no exhaust gases are emitted. Electric cars are on the cutting-edge of technology and are far more eco-friendly than cars with gasoline engines.

Major auto markets in Asia, Europe, and North America will shift to EVs (Electric Vehicles) within the next 10 years. China is the biggest automobile market in terms of number of cars sold. Because of the health problems caused by air pollution, China plans to stop selling gasoline cars and promote electric cars. European, American, and Japanese automakers are expected to make a similar move.

In 2009, the "i-MiEV" became the world's first mass-produced electric car. Currently, "Leaf" is the bestselling model in the global EV market. It would be wrong to assume, however, that these were the electric-car pioneers. In fact, electric cars first appeared in the mid-19th century. Although those electric cars showed great potential in terms of their speed, they were quite expensive and could only run for short distances due to their short battery lives.

The latest electric cars run on lithium-ion batteries that allow for longer, smoother, and quieter drives. If you have a "quick start" feature on your EV, you may feel as if you are being pushed back against the seat, a sensation similar to that experienced when taking off from the ground on a jet plane.

As more people turn to electric cars, demand for charging stations and electricity will also grow. Furthermore, as the number of EVs increases, a huge number of solar panels may have to be constructed in order to provide a clean and reliable supply of electricity.

(306 words)

(L. 1) pose 引き起こす　(L. 3) conventional 従来の　(L. 4) emission 放出　(L. 4) exhaust gas 排気ガス
(L. 5) cutting-edge 最新の　(L. 7) EV 電気自動車　(L. 8) automobile 自動車　(L. 13) currently 現在
(L. 14) pioneer 先駆者　(L. 18) lithium-ion battery リチウムイオン電池　(L. 20) sensation 感覚
(L. 22) charging station 充電スタンド　(L. 24) construct 建設する

**Exercise 1** 本文を読んで，下の質問に答えましょう。

1. What is the most important feature of an electric car?
   (A) An electric car uses less energy than a conventional car.
   (B) An electric car is equipped with the most advanced technology.
   (C) An electric car is powered by an electric motor and a gasoline engine.
   (D) We can drive the car without emitting harmful exhaust gases.

2. Why does China plan to promote electric cars?
   (A) Because electric cars are becoming popular.
   (B) Because the quality of electric cars is higher than that of gasoline cars.
   (C) Because air pollution is causing serious health problems.
   (D) Because the world's auto markets are moving to electric cars.

3. What does the passage suggest about the latest model of electric car?
   (A) That it will also require a small amount of gasoline.
   (B) That it will make it possible for us to enjoy a longer and more comfortable drive.
   (C) That the lack of charging stations will affect its performance.
   (D) That it will run off heavy batteries loaded into the front part of the car.

**Exercise 2** 次の各文が本文の内容に合っていればTを，合っていなければFを選びましょう。

1. 【T / F】 Electric cars are expected to help reduce air pollution since they have a unique feature known as the "Zero Emission Feature."
2. 【T / F】 China is recognized as the biggest electric car market, followed by Europe, and then North America.
3. 【T / F】 The first generation of electric cars sold well, though they were expensive and their batteries were poor.

## 🔵 電気自動車 🔵

電気自動車は排気ガスが出ないこと以外に，静かさと振動の少なさがその特徴です。エンジン音のような騒音は全くありません。そのため，歩行者に車の接近を知らせる警報音を出す装置が付けられています。車内では，信号で停止した時，隣の車のエンジン音や風の音が聞こえるほどです。最近では，電気自動車を利用した自動運転の技術開発競争が激化しています。現在，エコカーとして普及を促す政策が各国で推し進められています。

# Writing

**Exercise 1** 日本語に合うように，( ) 内に適切な語を書き入れましょう。

1. A growing (　　　　) for electric cars has become apparent recently.
   （最近，電気自動車への需要の高まりが明らかになってきています。）

2. Major automakers are trying to (　　　　) from gasoline cars to electric cars.
   （主要な自動車会社はガソリン車から電気自動車に変えようとしています。）

3. Lithium-ion batteries (　　　　) for longer and more comfortable drives.
   （リチウムイオン電池が長い快適な運転を可能にしています。）

**Exercise 2** ( ) 内の語を並べ替えて，英文を完成させましょう。

1. Electric cars are powered ( gasoline / by / electric / engines / not / motors / and / by ).
   （電気自動車はガソリンエンジンではなく電気モーターで動きます。）

   ..................................................................................................................

2. The world's first ( cars / sold / mass-produced / were / electric ) in 2009.

   ..................................................................................................................

3. More charging stations and ( cars / points / be / electric / necessary / electricity-supply / will / for ).

   ..................................................................................................................

# Speaking 次の表現を使って，パートナーと話す練習をしましょう。

> A: Are you doing anything to save energy?
> B: Yes, I recycle aluminum cans.
> A: Which energy source can best help reduce global warming?
> B: I think solar energy is most beneficial.

**Exercise** 日本語に合うように，英語で表現しましょう。

1. A: Are you doing anything to save energy?
   B: Yes, I _____?（不必要な電気を消す，LED 照明［LED lighting］を使用する）

2. A: Which energy source is most beneficial to prevent global warming?
   B: I think _____ is most beneficial.（水力発電［water power generation］，風力発電）

# Unit 15
# The Amazing Brain
驚異的な脳の働き

## 🔊 Listening  Warming up

◆ 意味のまとまり（チャンク）で展開を予測して聞く ◆
単語単位で聞き取ろうとせずに，ある程度の意味のまとまりでとらえるようにしましょう。下記の "/" がひとまとまりを表します。まとまりで読んでみましょう。

① Where did you / take her / last weekend?
② I took her / to the aquarium.

音声を聞く際に，どういう場面かを連想し，どのような言い回しが使われそうか推測し，自分が持っている背景知識と結び付けながらリスニングしましょう。

**Exercise 1**   CD を聴いて，何の説明か，その名前を日本語で（　）内に書き入れましょう。

A (　　　　　)　　　B (　　　　　)　　　C (　　　　　)

**Exercise 2**   CD を聴いて，最も適切な応答を一つ選びましょう。

1. (A) (B) (C)   2. (A) (B) (C)   3. (A) (B) (C)   4. (A) (B) (C)

**Exercise 3**   Opening Conversation を聴いて，下の質問に日本語で答えましょう。

1. Sayaka の次のクラスの教科は何ですか。

　　　　　　　　　　　　　　　　　　　　　　　　　　　　　　　　

2. そのクラスの宿題は何ですか。

## Reading 英文を読んで，質問に答えましょう。

76

The brain is an important part of the nervous system and a processing center coordinating all of the body parts. The human brain has a complex and well-developed neuron network to receive and send information. It commands hundreds of muscles so that we can walk, talk, and hold things. We also know that the brain controls all of the higher mental activities such as sensation and all of the thought processes connected with consciousness.

Human beings have the unique ability to communicate through language. Scientists have discovered that Wernicke's area and Broca's area, both of which are found in the brain's left hemisphere, are involved with language activities. Wernicke's area comprehends spoken and written words and sends the information to Broca's area. Broca's area adds grammatical processing and directs the motor area of the brain in order to stimulate the appropriate muscles for speaking and writing.

The various parts of the brain can vary in size depending on the individual. Research conducted on taxi drivers in London indicates that the drivers possess larger neurological areas for memory compared to other people. This shows that you can actually increase the size of certain areas of the brain through training. Brain activity may also vary among individuals. When listening to a song's rhythm or melody, a musician's brain activity may be different from that of a person who is not musically inclined.

Brain research has been able to progress because of recent technological breakthroughs. Thanks to the development of fMRI, scientists can now observe blood flow inside the brain. This instrument enables us to detect where activities like speaking, thinking, and dreaming take place inside the brain. What is presently known about the brain does not, however, cover all of the brain's amazing activities and capabilities. And for as long as scientists continue to explore its inner workings, the mystery of the human brain will never come to an end.

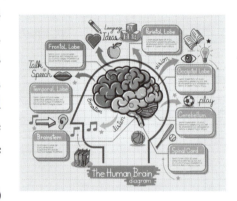

(318 words)

---

(L. 1) nervous system 神経系　　(L. 1) processing center 処理中枢　　(L. 2) well-developed 十分発達した
(L. 3) neuron 神経細胞　　(L. 5) sensation 感覚　　(L. 5) thought process 思考過程　　(L. 6) consciousness 意識
(L. 8) Wernicke's area ウェルニッケ野（感覚性言語野）　　(L. 8) Broca's area ブローカ野（運動性言語野）
(L. 9) left hemisphere（大脳の）左半球　　(L. 10) comprehend 理解する　　(L. 11) motor area 運動野
(L. 14) possess 所有する　　(L. 15) neurological 神経の　　(L. 19) inclined 素養がある　　(L. 21) breakthrough 進展
(L. 21) fMRI (functional magnetic resonance imaging) 機能的磁気共鳴断層撮影装置

**Exercise 1**　本文を読んで，下の質問に答えましょう。

1. Which of the following is a higher mental activity of the human brain?
   (A) The nervous system
   (B) Walking
   (C) Sensation
   (D) The neuron network

2. What function is Broca's area associated with?
   (A) It is associated with brain size.
   (B) Its function differs depending on the individual.
   (C) It is concerned with development of the left hemisphere of the brain.
   (D) It is associated with language activities.

3. What can we do with fMRI technology?
   (A) We can understand the development of scientific breakthroughs.
   (B) We can identify the activated parts of the brain when speaking or thinking.
   (C) Scientists can realize that the brain is a never-ending mystery.
   (D) We can understand that the more blood flow increases, the more activated our brain becomes.

**Exercise 2**　次の各文が本文の内容に合っていればTを，合っていなければFを選びましょう。

1. 【T / F】 The human brain controls hundreds of muscles in the body.

2. 【T / F】 Wernicke's area is in the right hemisphere and Broca's area is in the left hemisphere.

3. 【T / F】 A great deal is known to us about how the human brain functions, but not everything.

---

◯ 寝ている時は脳も活動していない？ ◯

デフォルトモードネットワーク (DMN) は，ぼーっとしている時の脳内ネットワークの一つで，意図的な活動をしている時の20倍活動すると言われています。人は睡眠状態の時に脳内の記憶を整理して，脳に定着させようとし，この時の領域はDMNの活動領域と一致しています。過去の記憶の呼び出しや，将来の展望を描いたりするのに重要な働きをしているとみられています。

# ✏️ Writing

**Exercise 1**　日本語に合うように，（　）内に適切な語を書き入れましょう。

1. The human brain has a set of functions like (　　　　　) and consciousness.
   （人間の脳は感情や意識のような一連の機能を持っています。）

2. Broca's area is (　　　　　) with grammar processing and the motor area for speaking and writing.
   （ブローカ野は文法処理や話したり，書いたりする運動野に関連しています。）

3. The instrument (　　　　　) us to detect changes in blood flow in the brain.
   （その装置のおかげで脳内の血流の変化を見つけることができます。）

**Exercise 2**　（　）内の語を並べ替えて，英文を完成させましょう。

1. Human beings are ( speak / other / with / through / to / each / able ) language.
   （人間は言葉を使って話すことができます。）

   ..................................................................................................................................

2. We can ( things / in / store / mind ) or recall events from the past.

   ..................................................................................................................................

3. Scientists ( investigate / of / will / the / continue / mysteries / to ) the human brain.

   ..................................................................................................................................

## 💬 Speaking　次の表現を使って，パートナーと話す練習をしましょう。

> A: I would like to ask you more about brain functions.
> B: Sure, how can I help you?
> A: I might join the party.
> B: That would be great!

**Exercise**　日本語に合うように，英語で表現しましょう。

1. A: I would like to ask you more about _____.　（課題，テスト，あなたの興味）
   B: Sure, how can I help you?

2. A: I might join _____.　（クラブ，ミーティング，旅行）
   B: That would be great!

# 付　録

## ①【母音】

　母音は，声道の形を変化させることで調節できます（図1）。口を大きく開けたり（「口の開き・広」），逆に小さく開けたり（「口の開き・狭」），舌の前の方を持ち上げたり（「舌の位置・前舌」），逆に後ろの方を持ち上げたり（「舌の位置・後舌」）して，色々な母音が出せます。特に，英語の母音は日本語の母音よりも口を縦にも横にも広げて使います。下の図を見ると日本語の母音は英語よりも狭い空間で発音していることが分かります。p.55には出てきていませんが，英語らしい音としてあいまい母音（schwa）があります。

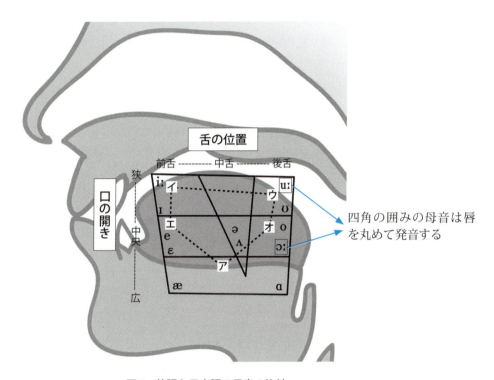

図1　英語と日本語の母音の比較

〈日本語と英語の違い〉

　左図は，口の開き具合に注目して5つの母音を整理したものです。英語の「ア」に似て聞こえる音は，日本語の「ア」よりも大きめに口を広げるのだということが分かります。そのため「ア」よりも気持ち広めの [ʌ]，もっと広げて「エ」の音を混ぜて [æ]，そして「ガパッ」と開けて [ɑ] といった具合です。

## ②【機能語と内容語】

　強アクセントと弱アクセントは品詞の違いにあります。強く発音される品詞と弱く発音される品詞について以下の表に整理しておきます。

| 内容語＝強アクセント | | 機能語＝弱アクセント | |
|---|---|---|---|
| 品詞 | 例 | 品詞 | 例 |
| 一般動詞 | go, do, study, listen | be 動詞 | is, am, are |
| 名詞 | Nagoya, Mary, flower, house | 人称代名詞 | I, you, he, she, we, they |
| 形容詞 | red, small, good, difficult | 助動詞 | do, can, may, must, should |
| 副詞 | yesterday, now, slowly | 前置詞 | to, in, on, at, for, with |
| 疑問詞 | what, when, where, why, how | 冠詞 | a, an, the |
| 指示詞 | this, that | 接続詞 | and, but, that |
| 数詞 | one, two, three | 関係詞 | that, who, which |

　原則としては，上記のように分類できますが，強調や対比をする場合，通常は弱アクセントの単語が強形を取ることがあります。例えば，有名なリンカーンの演説のセリフ "government **of** the people, **by** the people, **for** the people" では，前置詞の対比が重要となるため，of，by，for が強く発音されます。

③【弱形】

　英単語を見ると一語一語丁寧に強形で読みたくなりますが，文中では弱形も存在します。弱形になるのは，一般的に機能語です。機能語は文法的な機能としては重要ですが，意味的に重要ではないので，基本的に文中でははっきりと発音されません。他に重要な情報を伝えるためには，意識して弱く・あいまいに発音するということも必要です。

| 単語 | 強形 | 弱形 |
| --- | --- | --- |
| the | ði | ðə ðɪ |
| and | ænd | n̩ ən ənd |
| his | hɪz | ɪz |
| her | hɜː | ə |
| your | jɔː | jə |
| he | hiː | hɪ hi ɪ i |
| she | ʃiː | ʃɪ ʃi |
| him | hɪm | ɪm |
| for | fɔː(r) | fə(r) |
| of | ɒv | əv |
| have | hæv | əv |
| has | hæz | əz |

1. He <u>must</u> go to the bank and cash a check.　（マァス）
2. Jane looks pale.  Take <u>her</u> to the hospital.　（アー）
3. rock'n'roll ← rock <u>and</u> roll　（ロックンロール）

## ④【イントネーション】

イントネーションには，音の高さ低さ，音の強弱，長さが関連しています。この音の変化によって，話者の態度，意図，感情，特性など様々な情報を伝えます。例えば，Excuse me では次のような意味の違いがあります。音声と表記のイメージに合わせて発音しましょう。

### Excuse me のイントネーションの意味

 78

① Excuse me.（下げ調子）ごめんなさい，すみません！（謝罪）

② Excuse me?（上げ調子）もう一度言ってください（聞き返し）

③ Excuse me?（下げて上げる調子）すみません（人を呼び止める）

外国語学習者が「ごめんなさい」の意味で言ったつもりが，誤って上げ調子で言ってしまうと，英語話者は誤りと気づかないので，不快な気持ちにさせてしまいます。また，呼びかけるときは，一度 Excuse で下げてから me 上げますので，大げさに発音するくらいに発音してみましょう。

### 付加疑問文の場合

断定するときは下げ調子で，不確定や疑問のときは上げ調子で発音します。

④ It's snowing, isn't it?（ね，見たとおり）　　⑤ It's snowing, isn't it?（確信はないけれど…）

### 疑問詞を用いた疑問文（Wh 疑問文，How）の場合

疑問文は上げ調子ばかりではありません。疑問詞の What，How などは基本的に下げ調子です。

⑥ What is it ?　　　　　　　　　　⑦ How are you?

## ⑤【リンキング】

英語は句，節，文のように単位が長くなると音が連結し，一語で発音するときと異なります。 79
ここでは，文内で音のつながりを意識して練習しましょう。CD で正確な音声を確認しましょう。

1. I can stop by your office this evening to p<u>ck it u</u>p.　　　（ピキッタッ）

2. We had to p<u>ut it o</u>ff until tomorrow afternoon.　　　（プリトッ）

3. I'd like to have a c<u>up of</u> coffee.　　　（カッポォ）

| 著作権法上、無断複写・複製は禁じられています。 |

| | |
|---|---|
| Amazing Visions of the Future —Aspects of Human Activity— | [B-888] |

国際社会への英語の扉 —インプットからアウトプットで学ぶ四技能—

| | | |
|---|---|---|
| 1 刷 | 2019年 4月 1日 | |
| 7 刷 | 2024年 4月 10日 | |
| 著 者 | 伊與田　洋之 | Hiroyuki Iyoda |
| | 赤塚　麻里 | Mari Akatsuka |
| | 土居　峻 | Schun Doi |
| | 梶浦　眞由美 | Mayumi Kajiura |
| | マリキット G. マナラング | Marikit G. Manalang |
| | 室　淳子 | Junko Muro |
| 発行者 | 南雲　一範　Kazunori Nagumo | |
| 発行所 | 株式会社　南雲堂 | |
| | 〒162-0801　東京都新宿区山吹町361 | |
| | NAN'UN-DO Co., Ltd. | |
| | 361 Yamabuki-cho, Shinjuku-ku, Tokyo 162-0801, Japan | |
| | 振替口座：00160-0-46863 | |
| | TEL: 03-3268-2311（営業部：学校関係） | |
| | 　　　03-3268-2384（営業部：書店関係） | |
| | 　　　03-3268-2387（編集部） | |
| | FAX: 03-3269-2486 | |
| 編集者 | 丸小　雅臣／伊藤　宏実 | |
| 組　版 | 橋本　佳子 | |
| 装　丁 | NONdesign | |
| 検　印 | 省　略 | |
| コード | ISBN978-4-523-17888-0　C0082 | |

Printed in Japan

E-mail　nanundo@post.email.ne.jp
URL　https://www.nanun-do.co.jp/